ERNEST CHAUSSON

Ernest Chausson in 1895. *Courtesy of Jean Gallois.*

ERNEST CHAUSSON

The Man and His Music

Ralph Scott Grover

Lewisburg: Bucknell University Press
London: Associated University Presses

© 1980 by Associated University Presses, Inc.

Associated University Presses, Inc.
Cranbury, New Jersey 08512

Associated University Presses
Magdalen House
136-148 Tooley Street
London SE1 2TT, England

Library of Congress Cataloging in Publication Data

Grover, Ralph Scott, 1917-
Ernest Chausson, the man and his music.

Bibliography: p.
Includes Index.
1. Chausson, Ernest, 1855-1899.   2. Composers—
France—Biography.
ML410.C455G76   780'.92'4 [B]   77-74404
ISBN 0-8387-2128-2

To my wife, Frances,
who throughout this long and
sometimes trying project has been
most patient and understanding,
I dedicate this book in love and gratitude.

Contents

Acknowledgments

In a book almost wholly devoted to analyses of a composer's music, it is virtually axiomatic that most of the biographical details, together with such items as the listing of his complete works, will have been drawn from already published sources. That is true in this case, and it is with pleasure that I acknowledge my indebtedness to Messrs. Barricelli and Weinstein, and Gallois, whose books on Chausson provided much useful information and material. In addition, I thank M. Gallois for his kindness to me in Paris, where we enjoyed fruitful discussions concerning various phases of Chausson's life and career.

I am indebted to Mme Julia, Chausson's now deceased daughter, for kindly receiving me in her Versailles home, where I had the privilege of examining correspondence and admiring the delicate pastels painted by the composer; and to her daughter-in-law for taking the time to make this visit possible. I also wish to thank M. François Lesure, Curator of Music at the *Bibliothèque Nationale,* for presenting me with his valuable article *Claude Debussy, Ernest Chausson et Henri Lerolle.*

In London, the late Edward Lockspeiser very kindly made himself available for discussions of the Chausson-Debussy relationship.

Last but not least, I wish to thank Lafayette College for granting me a leave of absence to conduct much of the research necessary for the writing of this book.

I would like to thank the following publishers for permission to quote material under copyright:
Éditions Gallimard, for permission to quote the poem (actually used by Mallarmé to address the envelope of a letter

to Chausson) from Stéphane Mallarmé, *Vers de circonstance,* (c) Éditions Gallimard-Bibliothèque de la Pléiade (1965).

Éditions Seghers, for permission to quote from Jean Gallois, *Ernest Chausson: L'Homme et son oeuvre* (Paris: Éditions Seghers, 1967).

International Music Company for permission to reprint from *Chausson: 20 Songs for Voice and Piano,* edited by Sergius Kagen (© 1952), excerpts from the following: "Nocturne," "Nanny," "Printemps triste," "Nos Souvenirs," "Le Temps des lilas," "La Chanson bien douce," "L'Aveu," "La Caravane," "Dans la forêt du charme et de l'enchantement," and "Chanson Perpétuelle." Also from this volume, excerpts from Edith Braun's translations of the French poems of the following songs: "Les Papillons," "Nos Souvenirs," "La Dernière Feuille," "Chanson d'Ophélie," "La Chanson bien douce," and "La Caravane."

Also to reprint from *Debussy: 43 Songs for Voice and piano,* edited by Sergius Kagen (© 1951 and 1961), an excerpt from "C'est l'Extase langoureuse."

University of Oklahoma Press, for permission to quote from *Ernest Chausson: The Composer's Life and Works,* by Jean-Pierre Barricelli and Leo Weinstein. Copyright 1955 by the University of Oklahoma Press.

ERNEST CHAUSSON

1

The Background

ERNEST Amédée Chausson was born January 20, 1855, in Paris of wealthy parents. The father, Prosper, had acquired a modest fortune as a contractor during the years when Baron Haussmann designed and built the great Parisian boulevards; the composer later inherited this fortune, which enabled him to live a life of ease and refinement. Because of the deaths of their first two children, the parents showed unusual concern for Ernest, had him privately tutored at home, and so far protected him from the normal contacts of childhood as to develop in him an unnatural introspection and melancholy, which he only partially overcame in later life. "This relative solitude, along with the reading of a few morbid books, caused me to acquire another fault: I was sad without quite knowing why but firmly convinced that I had the best reason in the world for it."[1] This passage is quoted from a letter to Mme de Rayssac, whom he affectionately addressed as "godmother" and who exercised a strong influence over him during his youth; she advised him in matters pertaining to his choice of a career as well as in personal problems. She and her husband, the poet Saint-Cyr de Rayssac, who died in 1874, are the subjects of a glowing tribute by Anatole France.[2] Each was highly cultured and Mme de Rayssac was talented in both music and painting. It was at her Monday evening salons at 19 Rue Servandoni, near the Luxembourg Gardens and in the shadow of St. Sulpice, that Chausson's discriminating tastes in literature, painting, and music were nurtured, although these tastes had been previously fostered by Léon Brethous-Lafargue, the perceptive and unusual tutor engaged by the Chaussons for their son.

Brethous-Lafargue, sought after for his culture, tastes, and refinement, carried the youth far beyond the acquisition of book-learning. He was, in the words of Jean Gallois, "a true educator. . . . Explication of the great classical works, frequenting of literary and musical circles, long visits in Parisian museums thus contributed to developing very early in the child not only an acute perception but also the taste for beauty in all its forms."[3] He appears to have introduced Chausson to Mme de Rayssac and her circle when the youth was about fifteen. Among the frequent visitors to this salon were the painters Fantin-Latour and Odilon Redon, both of whom Chausson met in 1874. Redon, aged thirty-four, was to become his lifelong friend. After Chausson's death he undertook in 1901 as a memorial to his friend the decoration of the small music salon of Mme Chausson. He also executed a charcoal sketch of Chausson, a reproduction of which can be seen in Gallois's *Franck*. Roseline Bacou relates how the two friends were drawn together by a "passion for music, particularly Beethoven and Schumann." They performed duets together, Redon playing the violin, Chausson the piano. "Little notes addressed to 'Monsieur Odilon Redon, symphonic painter' fluttered to the Boulevard Montparnasse," proposing encores.[4] Other painters often seen at Mme de Rayssac's were her teacher Chenavard, official portraitist of the Tuileries; Louis Antoine Riesener, painter of genre, religious, and historical subjects, as well as cousin and admirer of Delacroix; and his daughter, Mlle Rosalie Riesener, who was his pupil. The latter is one of two young ladies in Fantin-Latour's painting *La Leçon de dessin* (1879); the other is Mlle Eva Callimaki-Catargi, to whom Chausson dedicated "Hébé," sixth of the *Sept Mélodies* of

Op. 2. The painting depicts both ladies about to copy a Greek plaster.[5] Interestingly, "Hébé" is subtitled "Chanson grecque dans le mode phrygien." A separate portrait of Mlle Calli-maki-Catargi was done by Fantin-Latour in 1881.

Though he was attracted equally by all of the arts, it was apparently some time before Chausson decided which one to pursue professionally. He was talented in painting; evidence supporting this fact exists in the form of perhaps a hundred sketches done in delicate pastel shades. They were examined by the present author in the Versailles home of the late Mme Julia, Chausson's youngest daughter. A reproduction of one may be seen here and in Gallois's *Chausson*. It was the composer's lifelong custom to record the many landscapes seen during his "incessants déplacements."[6] Chausson's literary ability is demonstrated by his libretto to *Le Roi Arthus,* the opera that occupied him from 1886 to 1895. He also wrote around 1877 a novel entitled *Jacques,* but because he destroyed it soon thereafter there is no way to judge its quality.

Music, however, was the art that attracted Chausson more than any of the others; his associations with musicians at Mme de Rayssac's salon and his study of the piano were powerful influences in his final decision to become a composer. However, his plans could materialize (if, indeed, at all) only after his father's desire for him to graduate in law had been satisfied. Accordingly, Chausson obtained his baccalaureate March 12, 1875, and his license April 24, 1876. Having thus satisfied his father, he reached an understanding with his parents concerning a career in music. In the fall of 1879, after a short summer trip to Munich, where he attended a performance of *Tristan und Isolde* and met, apparently for the first time, a "jeune musicien de beaucoup de talent," Vincent d'Indy,[7] Chausson became a pupil of both Massenet and Franck at the Paris Conservatoire. Another short visit to Germany followed in the summer of 1880, at which time Chausson heard *Tristan* again. Late in that year he decided to study exclusively with Franck; his formal studies with the latter were concluded in 1883.

On June 20, 1883, in the Church of St. Augustin, Chausson married Jeanne Escudier, a talented pianist and sister-in-law of the painter Henri Lerolle. He had first been introduced to her at Mme de Rayssac's salon by Alfred Lenoir, a sculptor. She was a constant source of inspiration and encouragement throughout their married life. Five children were born of their union. The couple moved into the large, spacious house at 22 Boulevard de Courcelles that had been occupied since the summer of 1875 by Chausson's parents. The furnishings and luxurious appointments of this house, here described by Camille Mauclair, one of Chausson's close friends, deserve mention:

> His home was a marvel of taste and art, graced by Henri Lerolle with delicate decorations: a gallery where the Odilon Redons and the Degas were neighbors with the Besnards, the Puvis [de Chavannes] and the Carrières. He lived there among the high, closed drapes, the pianos, the sober furniture, the scores and the books. . . . The friends who came often to spend the evening were the premier artists of our time. In the spacious study, shadowed, withdrawn from the noise of life, some faces were faintly illuminated in the half-lights of the shaded lamps. Above everyone, the large family portrait by Eugène Carrière reared its tall silhouettes, the man strong and gentle, a large white form of a woman bending down, the smiling likenesses of children. This was a pictorial record of delightful moments around a score.[8]

A more detailed and vivid description of some of the paintings follows:

> Here is a Corot from Italy, pearly, a composition of the southern sun. And here, near it, are some dancers of Degas, supple, ready to leap into the air; and *l'Homme au chapeau* which is one of the most fascinating works of art by Degas

the portraitist. Here, by Renoir, is his son Coco, only just indicated and yet so recognizable. Here is a Lerolle, there an Albert Besnard painting the couple's features at the piano. Here is Maurice Denis and his Christian zeal. There is Carrière. . . .[9]

From the above passages it can be seen that Chausson was a careful and discriminating collector. Of course, he purchased these paintings at a time when their value was nowhere near what it is today, but he must have been aware of their superior quality, as well as proud that some of them were by close personal friends. Also to be seen were works by Delacroix, Courbet, Manet, Gauguin, and Vuillard. The size and worth of Chausson's collection may be ascertained by studying the list of paintings sold June 5, 1936, by Mme Chausson; this list, presented below as Appendix B, includes certain paintings by Redon, Vuillard, and others presumably retained by the family and not offered for sale—at least not then. In addition to Lerolle's work, Chausson's home was also decorated by Maurice Denis, one of the Nabi painters and a close personal friend of the composer. These decorations took the form of three ceilings: *Avril,* 1894; *Le Printemps,* 1896; and *Terrase de Fiesole,* 1898.[10]

A veritable galaxy of late nineteenth-century figures in the arts flowed in and out of this mansion through the years. Among the painters and sculptors were Besnard, Carrière, Manet, Redon, Degas, Renoir, Denis, Vuillard, and Rodin. Poets and writers were represented by Mallarmé, Henri de Régnier, Gérard d'Houville (who became Mme de Régnier in 1896); the young Gide; the caustic and witty music critic Henri Gauthier-Villars, who adopted the name "Willy" among others; his wife Colette, later to become famous in her own right (their marriage was terminated by divorce in 1906); Camille Mauclair; and Maurice Bouchor. Among the composers were Franck and the "Franckistes" d'Indy, Duparc, Bordes, Bréville, Ropartz, Magnard, and Benoît.

Other composers were Fauré, Dukas, Chabrier, Debussy, Albeniz, Bonheur, Satie, Messager, Chevillard, Lazzari, Koechlin, and Samazeuilh.

There were many performers, some already famous, others who would be. If we divide them into categories we find among the violinists Ysaÿe, Thibaud, Parent, Crickboom; pianists, Pugno, Mme Bordes-Pène, Cortot, Risler. Singers were represented by Georgette Leblanc, the wife of Maurice Maeterlinck; the opera singer Mme Jeanne Raunay; Thérèse Page; Claire Croiza; the great Wagnerian tenor and close friend of Chabrier, Ernest van Dyke; and Maurice Bagès, whose diction as interpreter of French *mélodies* was said to have been "impeccable."[11] Also the critics Pierre Lalo, André Hallays, and Robert Brussel.

Chausson was also seen at gatherings of brilliant people outside his own home. J. P. Crespelle gives us some details:

> There existed a refined and cultured society which, if it patronized the traditional painters, interested itself now and then in the innovators. The "movers" in this circle were the Comtesse de Saint Marceaux, Valtesse de la Bigne, la Comtesse Greffulhe [the model for Proust's Duchesse de Guermantes] and Mme Strauss. The first, more particularly oriented towards music—as it would be later with Madeleine Lemaire—gave the musical soirées. . . . Fauré, Messager, Dukas, Chausson, Chabrier, and also Albert Roussel and Florent Schmitt were the frequenters of these gatherings.[12]

Princesse Edmond de Polignac, who grew up in the salon "system" and later maintained a salon of her own at which Chausson was a guest, remarks that

> One of the most interesting Salons I ever knew in Paris was that of the sculptor, René de St. Marceaux and his wife. They lived in the Boulevard Malesherbes, and every Friday there used to be an informal reception, after an excellent dinner. Nobody who had not exhibited a piece of sculpture or a picture, or who was not a composer, a

scientist or an inventor would ever be invited to these gatherings, to which no simple "mondain" or mere social star was admitted.[13]

After describing how she had met Debussy and Ravel there and calling attention to Debussy's appearance at that time, she continues:

> Claude Debussy and André Messager used to play *à quatre mains* many scores that delighted us. . . . We never tired of hearing them play.
>
> Among those who crowded round the piano were Gabriel Fauré, Chabrier, Vincent d'Indy, Colette (who was then thin and frail and newly married to Gauthier-Villars— "Willy"—whose criticisms of the Sunday concerts, signed *Lettres de l'Ouvreuse,* were feared by all the young composers), Jean-Louis Forain, [a noted cartoonist], Pierre Louÿs, Chausson and sometimes Sargent [the fashionable American portrait painter] and Claude Monet. Music, books and pictures were discussed among them all, until the night was almost spent.[14]

Another important salon almost certainly attended by Chausson was that of Mme Arthur Fontaine, wife of a prominent industrialist and sister-in-law of the composer. Among those who came to her musical soirées near Les Invalides were Debussy, Valéry, Gide, the poet Francis Jammes, and Paul Claudel. One of Vuillard's warmest interior paintings, done about 1900, shows Mme Fontaine standing across the room in front of her window.[15]

Chausson's life from 1883 to 1899, the year of his sudden and tragic death, was filled with the details associated with the composition and performance of his music. Included in these activities were numerous trips and summer vacations, during which he wrote many of his compositions; his habit was to spend the winter in Paris polishing the works he had composed during spring and summer vacations in the country. He detested the noise of Paris and spent as little time there as possible. Some of these trips were to the south of

France where, at Cibourre, for example, much work was done on the Symphony in B-flat. Other sojourns were to Italy; at least one to Spain where, in 1896, the composer conducted a performance of his symphony at Barcelona; to Belgium, in connection with performances of various works; to Germany, including summer excursions to Bayreuth; and holidays in the country not far from Paris.

It was during one of the latter respites in the summer of 1899 that Chausson met his death on June 10. He had rented a villa at Limay near Mantes that, according to Maurice Denis, had once been occupied by Corot.[16] Gallois supplies us with the details:

> On the tenth of June, around six-thirty, putting his score aside for a moment [the String Quartet in C minor, later carried by d'Indy to a logical conclusion shortly after Chausson's stopping point] he called his eldest daughter, Étiennette, and departed with her on the familiar road to the neighboring railroad station, there to meet his wife and his other children who were returning from Paris. [Each was riding a bicycle]. Being more agile, the young cyclist took the lead and, turning around, failed to see her father. She then retraced her steps; but she had the horrible [experience] of discovering the musician lying at the foot of the carriage entrance, his temple crushed. He was killed instantly.[17]

Gallois immediately follows this account with an effort to probe the cause of "ce stupide accident." He questions whether over-fatigue, accentuated by the heat of the afternoon, was at fault. Or was it Chausson's lack of skill on a bicycle? Tending to support this latter theory is a letter describing Chausson's funny and awkward appearance on his bicycle. Gallois points out that the route he and his daughter took was very familiar and that, contrary to what had been thought, the path descended in a relatively easy grade.[18] Denis also speaks of the normal course in which the tragedy occurred and goes on to remark on the force with which

Chausson's head was crushed against the wall.[19] Edward Lockspeiser terms the accident "mysterious" and refers to it as "following a period of acute depression, and in which there may well have been a suicidal element."[20] Needless to say, Chausson's family and friends were completely stunned by the tragedy. The funeral services were conducted at the Church of Saint-François de-Sales on June 15. "An enormous crowd of musicians, writers, artists, friends [in fact, many of those mentioned earlier as having been guests at 22 Boulevard de Courcelles] had come to offer a final homage." Camille Benoît, one of the Franckistes, delivered the farewell remarks.[21] Burial was in Père-Lachaise Cemetery.

In addition to the String Quartet in C minor mentioned above, the following projects were "more or less advanced," according to Gustave Samazeuilh: "an outline of a drama on an underlying idea whose intense lyricism might have been well suited to the nature of his talent, some overtures for orchestra, a sonata for piano and violin, and a second symphony to which at first he seemed to want to devote himself."[22]

Chausson is a perfect example of an artist whose temperament and personality shaped to a great degree the types, quality, and quantity of his total output. As we have already seen, he mingled with the greatest figures in the arts of his time. It seems highly unlikely that the various artistic causes and movements in which these people were involved and which made Paris an artistic and intellectual ferment during the closing years of the century would, or could, have left Chausson unaffected. They undoubtedly helped to shape some attitudes to which he also brought certain natural characteristics. The interaction of these elements, together with the wealth and leisure to which he was accustomed, combined to produce a body of music that can be considered quite aside from the influences of others on his music. To put it another way, the matter of influences—so often mentioned when Chausson's music is discussed (usually superficially)—

is subsumed in a larger scheme dictated by extramusical considerations. These latter have been ignored as far as any attempt to trace their nonmusical origins is concerned. Adjectives like *elegiac, aristocratic,* and *polished* have been applied by critics who have never investigated the circumstances that gave rise to their use. And each of these adjectives is largely correct as characterizations for much of Chausson's music; each has its source in that subtle combination of personal qualities and the artistic milieu in which Chausson lived and worked.

Two main ingredients of Chausson's character were, according to documented evidence, an innate goodness, and a generosity marked by real self-effacement. The first is mentioned by the composer's brother-in-law, Henri Lerolle, who in a letter to Denis described him as having "one of the most beautiful characters of any man I have ever known."[23] This view is supported by Gustave Samazeuilh, composer, critic, friend, and pupil of Chausson: "numerous friends whom he was pleased to bring together in his friendly home have not forgotten the exquisite goodness of his spirit."[24]

As for Chausson's generosity, it was proverbial. He used his fortune to help deserving but impecunious fellow composers with the understanding that his name would not be revealed.[25] He was even self-effacing before men who were ungrateful for his help and "was the first to rejoice in their success."[26] Camille Mauclair mentions the composer's belief that he should come to the aid of a "confrère having more need than he of publicity or money."[27] Also, as the secretary for ten years of the Société Nationale de Musique, he was in an excellent position to help struggling composers by insuring performances of their scores. In one such instance, Ravel's overture *Shéhérazade* was performed May 27, 1899, at the Société when Chausson withdrew one of his own works in favor of the younger man. Two further recipients of his generosity were Albeniz and Debussy: I shall have occasion later to detail the aid accorded the latter.

Chausson's generous nature was not restricted to helping struggling younger men; it was demonstrated in his relationships with composers of his own age or even older. A case in point concerns his friend Chabrier. Princesse de Polignac relates the details:

> When I suggested giving a concert in Paris in which the principal parts of *Gwendoline* would be heard, with a reduced orchestra and chorus, Chabrier could not believe his ears, and at once asked most of his musical friends such as Vincent d'Indy, Gabriel Fauré, and Ernest Chausson to take part in it, and in a letter to van Dyke he speaks of this performance in which he played the piano, Gabriel Fauré the harmonium, and Vincent d'Indy the *timbales* or tympani. [What Chausson's part in the venture was is not indicated].
> It was a great success, although the public naturally thought the music extraordinarily modern and advanced . . . other works by d'Indy and Chausson, now well known, were heard then for the first time.[28]

After Chabrier's death in 1894, a short but warmly generous tribute written by Chausson appeared in company with others contributed by various composers and poets.[29]

In a letter of 1890 to his friend Paul Poujaud, a lawyer and ardent devotee of the arts, Chausson expressed concern for Fauré: "Send me news about Fauré's health. Don't you think that some possibility must be found to let him spend a quiet winter outside of Paris? Consider the most fantastic means of arranging that. . . ."[30]

Another trait, strongly negative in character, had unfortunate consequences on Chausson's life and work: his extreme self-doubt. There are various documented sources corroborating this, not the least of which is by Chausson himself; several examples appear below. In each instance the self-doubt is linked with current projects either planned or being written.

> It only remains to be seen whether I shall have the power within me of expressing what I am feeling. As long as I am only thinking of it, I am full of confidence; once I have a pencil in my hand, I feel like a very small boy.[31]

And again:

> I am beginning to have a little confidence, not in what I am doing but in what I shall do with this drama (*Arthus*). . . . How light-hearted I feel, my dear friend. It infuriates me, but that changes nothing. My feelings are more stable, fortunately. . . . I am entangled in a lot of confused ideas, which run into one another, jostle each other, one chasing away the other, and sometimes returning a little while later. I understand nothing about anything. I feel in myself the most contradictory things. . . . With me that lasts for a long time; it only gets worse. I have yet a few little lights left and I feel so many winds blowing in all directions which threaten to extinguish them.[32]

In connection with the Symphony there are these desperate words:

> since being here I have been working like a slave and I am stuck at one measure! I have tried to stop, impossible. I return to my paper as to a vice. To do anything else, also impossible. I cannot think and think only of that one measure. So I loathe it; I hurl insults at myself, I hit myself with my fists. As you can imagine, that helps a lot. Most horrible of all, what I am about to write is very good. I don't tell you that often about my music; this time I sincerely believe that it is good. No doubt about it, it is even too good for me; I had a lucky beginning and now I find myself afloat without being able to continue, unwilling to give up, a prey of frenzy. I play over incessantly what I have written, always hoping that a good inspiration will enable me to get by the fatal measure, and it is always the same thing, and I begin again and stop once more. Imag-

ine, I stopped just a moment ago. It was for the twentieth time today. It is like that every day. It will be like that again tomorrow. I no longer dare get up in the morning, thinking of the frightful day I am going to spend.[33]

One final excerpt in Chausson's own words follows:

I have told you little about my work this year. The reason is that I pass so often and so quickly through alternate stages of rage, gaiety, enthusiasm and despair that I find it preferable not to cast light on these shameful nuisances. Recounting them grants them too much importance. And, when my friends answer me, it always happens that my state of mind has changed and, if they speak of my "good work" at the moment when I am pulling my hair out, I howl and accomplish even less.[34]

Further self-documentation of Chausson's lack of confidence may be found in those letters where the overwhelming problem of Wagner's influence is cited and discussed; excerpts from these letters appear later.[35]

Chausson's self-doubts were also noted by his friends and associates. Mauclair observed them in connection with an incident at the first Paris performance of *Poème*, played by Ysaÿe at the Concerts Colonne on April 4, 1897. He and Chausson were backstage at the Théâtre Chatelet when, at the conclusion of the work, there was a great round of applause. Mauclair saw the utter stupefaction on Chausson's face and, as they descended the winding staircase together, he heard him remark, "I can't get over it!"[36] Samazeuilh also mentions how Chausson often doubted his own ideas and failed to recognize the importance of formulating them without delay. He goes on to say that "his entire work bears traces of a constant aspiration towards an ideal never completely revealed."[37] It would appear to be no accident that, as Gallois observes, Chausson found the following lines from Wolfram von Eschenbach's *Parzival* producing a "faithful echo" in his own soul:

Wohnt der Zweifel nah dem Herzen
Das bringt bess'res Weh der Seele.[38]

When doubt dwells in the heart
It brings much pain to the soul.

Chausson's lack of self-confidence may have been an out-growth of another characteristic trait: that of living a life deep within himself. Mauclair speaks of him as having "always the appearance of rising from the middle of a dream and taking a step toward real life." He adds that "he was one of those who concern themselves all their lives with their inner life."[39] Of course the more deeply one retires within himself to find the real life there rather than in the outer world, the less confidence in oneself there is likely to be when the materialization of inner dreams is attempted and the problems of daily life are faced. Chausson's wealth obviated the necessity of composition as a means of livelihood—a fact that cannot be denied even though he worked diligently and relentlessly on his musical works. That fact, and the mansion at 22 Boulevard de Courcelles with its huge study protected from the outside world, lined with books, and hung with favorite paintings, certainly fostered an interior, sheltered world of the spirit. Even some of the paintings he had acquired tend to strengthen this conclusion. Odilon Redon, his close friend mentioned earlier, painted pictures of a visionary world; Arthur Symons has, in fact, referred to him as "a French Blake."[40] In addition to the red chalk portrait of himself, Chausson owned at least two works of Redon—the charcoal sketch "L'Ange déchu" of 1885/86 and the oil painting "La Vierge d'aurore" of 1895; both of these are highly imaginative and show us Redon's inner world.

However, Chausson's tendency to withdraw into himself was not peculiar to him, for it was also one of the distinguishing marks of Stéphane Mallarmé's Symbolisme, a movement with which Chausson was intimately connected through his friendships with Mallarmé and his circle.[41] The problems of living in the inner world of the spirit and imagination as opposed to involvement in the outer world of action receive much attention in scholarly studies of Symbolism; there they emerge as some of the central issues of the French intellectual and artistic life of the *fin de siècle.*[42]

These problems form the very heart of the important novel *Le Soleil des morts,* a very penetrating study of the relationship between Mallarmé and his daughter Geneviève. Written by Mauclair and published in 1898, the book is considered to be an authentic exegesis of French Symbolism. It presents the two extremes of activity and inactivity, creativity and impotence, in terms of the most brilliant figures in the arts, all of whom have fictitious names.[43] Chausson (Rodolphe Méreuse) appears three times in minor situations only: he is pictured as being in Mallarmé's (Calixte Armel's) rue de Rome apartment, where he plays the piano for Mallarmé and his daughter Geneviève (Sylvaine); he comforts and reassures Debussy (Claude-Eric de Harmor) just before the latter's pieces are played for the first time at the Concerts Lamoureux; after the concert, he appears at Debussy's side in the foyer. At no time does Chausson speak or enter any of the conversations, a fact perhaps significant in view of the author's dedication of the novel to him. For Mauclair seems to have deliberately de-emphasized Chausson by placing him in minor situations where no conversation was necessary. Thus he is made to appear almost neutral—not in a derogatory sense as having no opinions worth recording but in a positive way as being unaffected by the extremes. And extremes there are, for Mallarmé represents intellectual and artistic refinements of an incredibly tenuous sort, where there is literally nothing to grasp, while the opposite side of intense revolutionary activity is portrayed (more in Mauclair's imagination than in reality) by Émile Zola (Claude Pallat). The novel finally becomes a chronicle of the struggle between these two opposites. Mauclair's dedication seemingly reveals an ultimate judgment concerning Chausson, for it would appear that the honor is meant to imply a balance in Chausson's life between the two extremes. As partial support for this theory, there is Mauclair's remark that Chausson worked very hard in his efforts to overcome his "latent defeatism."[44] However, merely to accept Mauclair's possible judgment as it is implied in his dedication is too facile a solution to the problems created by Chausson's lack of self-confidence and his tendency to live in an interior world. That Chausson was aware of the extremes set forth in *Le Soleil des morts* and attempted to strike a balance between them is probably true, but his success (if any) in the struggle seems to have been conditioned both by his own nature and by the aesthetics inherent in Symbolism, some of which were strong contributors to the prevailing *Zeitgeist* in France during the closing years of the nineteenth century. By examining Symbolist aesthetics more closely, we shall be in a better position to judge what effect, if any, the underlying currents of this literary movement had on Chausson's life and music. I begin this examination with some passages from the studies of Symbolism already cited, for they not only explain the basic aesthetics of the movement but also reveal some of the atmosphere surrounding it.

As Bowra explains it, "against this scientific Realism [i.e., the Realism of Zola and other novelists like him] the Symbolists protested, and their protest was mystical in that it was made on behalf of an ideal world which was, in their judgment, more real than that of the senses. It was not in any strict sense Christian . . . . It was a religion of Ideal Beauty, of 'le Beau' and 'l'Idéal.' "[45] In trying to create a poetry in terms of an ideal world, words were weighed and reweighed in an effort to find exactly the right one. A private symbol was attached to such words and the poetry became more and more abstract, obscure, and hermetic. "Symbolism, indeed, sometimes had the result of making poetry so much a private concern of the poet's that it turned out to be incommunicable to the reader."[46] Mallarmé, as the theoretician and consummate practitioner of Symbolism, felt that " 'Everything sacred which wishes to remain so is enveloped in mystery.' . . . Hence a *closed* poetry, its meaning at first hidden from the reader, is required."[47] Carrying this idea further, Mallarmé "believed that in poetry he might produce an effect so absolutely aesthetic that the understanding would almost be in abeyance. The sounds and associations would do all the work; the mere meaning of the words would not matter."[48] The result of such an aesthetic was, of course, isolation. "The public, finding itself despised and feeling that the new poetry was beyond its comprehension, turned to cruder authors. And the poets, cut off from the public, were forced back on themselves and deprived of the strength which may be found in streets and crowds."[49] Certainly another result of dealing with such tenuous material in the rarefied air of Symbolism may be observed in the following observation:

> Mallarmé was such a severe taskmaster, so hard on himself, and he probed his own mettle so deeply, that he was not able to produce more than a dozen great poems in his lifetime; in every case, a conflict arose between his love of the poem and the critical spirit that destroyed it while he was creating it. As a result, he spent his entire life working on his meager harvest of poetic survivals, polishing and repolishing them, and dreaming of the Great Work which was never to be written because the plane of perfection on which he placed it in his imagination forbade the possibility of its ever becoming a reality. When he could not find fulfillment in the creation of the perfect work, he transferred his aspirations to the discussion of poetry before the sympathetic audience he had gathered around him.[50]

Both implicit and explicit in Symbolist thought and practice was the idea of "ennui"—that vague, ill-defined discontent of mind and spirit, the weariness and languor so often associated with the overrefined. The word and the ideas behind it occur again and again in Symbolist poetry. Other frequently used words expressing the same discontent are *spleen* and *esprit bleu.* It is not appropriate here to explore how or even if these attitudes resulted from dealing habitually with elusive ultra-refinements of thought; it is enough to say that these attitudes colored the manner of living and the work of an entire generation of European artists, writers, and musicians. In the expression *fin de siècle* this escapism, boredom, weariness, and disillusion are understood and accepted as significant contributors to the *Zeitgeist.*

Chausson lived and worked in this climate and, in view of his personal characteristics described above—self-doubts, hesitations, tendencies toward withdrawal (mentally into himself, physically into his luxurious study)—it seems fair to say that he was affected by it and unable to escape its essentially negative influence. Although he never set any of Mallarmé's poetry,[51] he did set five of Maeterlinck's *Serres chaudes,* a poetic cycle full of obscurity and employing a private symbolism replete with "blue ennui," "blue dreams," and languorous images. Just why Chausson chose to set one poet and not the other is unclear, especially in view of the fact that both poets appear to be equally obscure. Musically, the effects of Maeterlinck's poems on the composer are apparent in terms of thicker texture and greater harmonic complexity. They may be said to be the immediate results of a Symbolist influence on Chausson, negative or positive according to one's point of view.[52] If one accepts the premise that the time-honored goal of a majority of French composers has been clarity and logic in musical expression, then one is forced to admit that this particular influence is negative.

Another more permanent and more negative influence on Chausson appears, however, to have resulted from the Symbolist aesthetic: the very atmosphere engendered by the movement. This atmosphere, referred to as *fin de siècle* and/or *décadence,* can be defined more accurately in nega-

tive rather than in positive terms. In the following quotations
the aura surrounding Symbolism is distilled into more definite language:

> One's great objection to the Symbolist school is its lack
> of curiosity about life. With perhaps the single exception of
> Viélé-Griffin [an American who, while never renouncing
> his citizenship, lived in France all of his adult life and
> became one of the most important Symbolist poets] (and
> it is this that gives his verse so special a savor), all were
> pessimists, renunciants, resignationists, "tired of the sad
> hospital" which the earth seemed to them—our "mo-
> notonous and unmerited fatherland," as Laforgue called
> it. Poetry had become for them a refuge, the only escape
> from the hideous realities; they threw themselves into it
> with a desperate fervor.
> Divesting life as they did of everything which they con-
> sidered mere vain delusion, doubting whether it were
> "worth living," it was not astonishing that they should
> have supplied no new ethic . . . but only an aesthetic.[53]

In Balakian's study of the Symbolist movement, she notes
how

> Mallarmé was drawn to the image of Hamlet as the symbol
> of the nonparticipant, whose sensibility and power to
> dream ran counter to the mediocrity of existence. He
> identified with this image, and thereafter there is a veri-
> table cult of Hamlet. . . .
> In Mallarmé's writings as well as in his personal be-
> havior, this "decadence," [between these two quotations
> Balakian notes that the words "decadent" and "decadence"
> are used in the literary and not in the moral sense] as we
> have seen is apparent in the overpowering "ennui" of his
> existence, translated into objects and projected upon char-
> acters, his preoccupation with the imponderable "gouffre"
> or "azur," the futility of thought that will be swallowed
> up in death, the impossibility of escape from the sense
> of temporality, the acute sensitivity, the tendency to re-
> duce life to inaction and the dream, the withdrawal from
> the mainstream, the cloistered look, the Hamlet gesture.[54]

Another appraisal of Symbolism that also stresses the latter's negative qualities follows:

> This almost total rejection of the world, common to a Mallarmé and a Moreau [a French artist (1826–1898) whose subjects were of a visionary and fantastic nature], so far from being necessarily the sign of superior greatness of soul, points rather to impotence. This is shown by the fact that what they oppose to the world, the goal to which they strive to escape has only negative value: the Idea, that idol to which they sacrifice everything, is an absence of Idea. And this non-Idea has no recognizable counterpart other than their own impotence, their own sterility.[55]

If any conclusions can be drawn from these quotations insofar as Chausson was affected by the Symbolist atmosphere therein described, it is that some of the same artistic impotence and "tendency to reduce life to inaction and the dream, the withdrawal from the mainstream" (such withdrawal expressed, perhaps, in Chausson's case by his almost constant movements from place to place) are observable in his life. We have already seen his tendency toward an interior life that certainly reinforces "inaction and the dream," and have noted how his appearance was that of someone "rising from the middle of a dream and taking a step toward real life." But an even more concrete resemblance to Symbolist practice as noted by the English author and critic Arthur Symons seems to apply to at least some of Chausson's music: "an over subtilizing refinement upon refinement."[56] There certainly was the opportunity and the leisure to over-refine, as Chausson's custom of polishing during the winter months in Paris the music he had written on spring and summer holidays elsewhere indicates. However, with respect to this problem of over-refinement, there is a difference between the conflict that in Mallarmé "arose between his love of the poem and the critical spirit that destroyed it while he was creating it" and the dilemma that beset Chausson. All things considered, the output of both was meager but, whereas Mallarmé's keen intellect seemed to inhibit him, Chausson often suffered some kind of mental paralysis during the creative process, a conclusion we can legitimately draw from the correspondence quoted earlier. Now it is entirely possible and, indeed, probable that these results— over-refinement and mental paralysis—originated in his own background, but to ignore the prevailing Symbolist winds would be to blind ourselves to the fact that external forces in sympathy with an artist's basic personality traits often reinforce such traits. Thus, an artist is a contributor to and a recipient of the *Zeitgeist* and, in the last analysis, cannot escape it.

The first person to attempt to explain the elegiac tone found in so much of Chausson's music is Jean Gallois. He shows that this quality was a direct outgrowth of some of the personal characteristics and shaping forces already referred to; in the present author's opinion he makes a strong case. First, of course, is the seriousness and gravity of Chausson's nature, encouraged, no doubt, by such factors as the death in 1865 of his elder brother, Eugène-Prosper, when Ernest was ten. Another powerful determinant was his association at Mme de Rayssac's salon with persons "older, richer in experience and knowledge than he."[57] More to the point, perhaps, is the fact that, owing to his varied artistic talents and consequent long hesitation to follow music professionally, there was the realization that he was not really and "uniquely a musician."[58] And of course his father's insistence on a law degree postponed the decision further. Chausson was a perfectionist but also enough of a realist to know that perfection was unattainable; this knowledge helped to inhibit him. He also was aware of his abilities and limitations. All of this was expressed in his correspondence as doubts, reproaches, and hesitations "that formed like a melancholy halo around his music."[59] Finally, an aura of sadness envelops Chausson's words to Mme de Rayssac when he speaks of "a moment of fear, not of death but of

Ernest Chausson and his parents. *Courtesy of Jean Gallois.*

Le Lac Marion (to the left Mme Chausson). From a collection of pastels drawn by Chausson. *Courtesy of Jean Gallois.*

Chausson's mansion at 22 Boulevard de Courcelles, Paris. *Photograph by the author.*

dying without having finished my task, without having done what I was called to do."[60] Of course it goes without saying that the melancholic and elegiac tone of many of the songs is a faithful reproduction of the type of poem the composer chose to set. But it is reasonable to suppose that the poems would not have been chosen unless they were in rapport with Chausson's nature.[61] And there are, of course, the Symbolists among his poets with their texts expressing the ennui, spleen, *esprit bleu,* and general malaise of the *fin de siècle.* With their moods Chausson obviously had some spiritual kinship or he would not have set them.

A very positive facet of Chausson's personality was his critical objectivity in all areas pertaining to the arts. Concerning literature, he possessed a large and varied library where, according to Samazeuilh, one could find the "most singular [no doubt in the sense of discriminating] works of all literatures: poems, critical or philosophical essays attested to the vast culture of his spirit."[62] Gallois mentions that Racine, Balzac, and Stendhal were preferences and that

> as for his contemporaries, there was scarcely a name that Chausson had not wished to know from Bouchor to Maeterlinck, from Pushkin to Tolstoy, from Verlaine to Gide. His correspondence was adorned with reflections made à propos one and the other, and it was observed that he had read, pen in hand and, most frequently less than six months after their appearance, works sometimes printed in editions of less than five hundred copies—like "Sagesse" of Verlaine—or works known only by professional literary men—like "Les Nourritures Terrestres" of the young André Gide, or certain translations of Russian works.[63]

Among the Russian authors was Turgenev, all of whose works Chausson owned. Although Turgenev visited Paris frequently and died on French soil in 1883, there is no evidence that he and Chausson ever met or corresponded. There is a human link between them, however, in the person of

Pauline Garcia-Viardot, the great singer whose remarkable career spanned the nineteenth century from George Sand to Brahms and Debussy. She was the devoted and intimate friend of Turgenev and was also, together with her husband, Louis Viardot, a close friend of the Chaussons.[64]

Poujaud, in summing up Chausson's literary tastes, said of him:

> Of rare culture, loving especially the Greek tragedies, the poets of India, the Breton cycles, Shakespeare, Chausson welcomed every new work where he found eternal beauty . . . great admirer of Mallarmé, he was the first to perceive Maeterlinck.[65]

Chausson's tastes in other cultural areas were equally broad yet discriminating. His collection of contemporary paintings has already been mentioned. Among earlier artists he was particularly fond of Rembrandt, Van Dyck, Fra Angelico, and Botticelli; probably only the limitation of his personal fortune prevented him from owning works by these men. He was also allied in terms of sympathies and friendships with a group of painters called the Nabis, a Hebrew word meaning "prophets."[66] Among these artists were Paul Sérusier, follower of Gauguin and the group's founder; Paul Ranson, K. X. Roussel; Edouard Vuillard and Pierre Bonnard, both of whom later achieved fame as two of the most important artists of the twentieth century; and Maurice Denis, close personal friend of Chausson. These men were all from eight to fifteen years younger than Chausson. That Vuillard was also a personal friend of Chausson may be inferred from an exchange of letters between Denis and Vuillard. In one, dated Rome, February 15, 1898, Denis asks Vuillard, "have you visited the Chaussons? They certainly count on it." On February 19 Vuillard replied by saying, "I have been to the Chaussons without finding them."[67] Perhaps we shall learn something of the relationship between Chausson and Vuillard when the latter's private journal, by terms of his will, becomes public in 1980. On the other hand, there may be nothing significant, for Vuillard was a very shy and reticent person.

It is difficult if not impossible to determine exactly what aspects of the Nabis particularly attracted Chausson. Like his, their interests were wide and varied with respect to the arts, philosophy, and religion. Perhaps the very breadth of their tastes and reading appealed to him more than any one phase, for such an attitude was undoubtedly in sympathy with his own habits of investigation.

According to Denis, he and Sérusier studied Plato's myth of the cave. In addition,

> Zarathustra's hymns and teachings in the Avesta were read besides Baudelaire, Verlaine, Mallarmé, Rimbaud, Villiers de l'Isle-Adam and Laforgue's introduction to Schopenhauer. They busied themselves with Buddhism and frequented the spiritualistic circle of the Rosicrucian movement; they engaged in the magic arts of the Kabbala and Swedenborg's Theosophy, and also visited the scholastic lectures of the Dominicans in the Faubourg St. Honoré. The Nabi Hermant, a concert pianist, played compositions of Wagner and Bach on a harmonium, and in Lamoureux' house Maeterlinck's *Sept Princesses* was staged as a marionette play.[68]

As for their work, "the influence of the Nabis was felt mainly in the sphere of the applied arts: printing, posters, book-illustration, tapestry, pottery, stained glass. They had a knack of breathing new life into dying crafts. They also had considerable influence on other artistic and cultural activities."[69] As for preferences in music, the Nabis favored that written by Pierre Hermant, a member of their group; Ernest Chausson; Henri Duparc; Vincent d'Indy; and Claude Debussy.[70] Later the same author observes that, although Chausson was on very intimate terms with Maurice Denis, he never joined the Nabis.[71] From this we may assume that he took no part in their formalities or in their journalistic endeavors.

The latter centered on *La Revue blanche,* an organ for the avant-garde founded in 1891 by Alfred, Alexandre, and Thadée Natanson, sons of a banker, while the formalities were of a ritualistic kind and are alluded to in the following passage:

> Their works apart, the Nabis were characterized by a certain schoolboy pretentiousness which came out in a liking for ritual meetings, nicknames, and a secret language. . . .
>
> As important as the secret language were the secret meetings. Every month [from 1888 until 1896] the Nabis ate a ritual meal in a bistro in the Passage Brady; the member chosen to give the address held a sculptured staff like a bishop's crozier [there follow descriptions of a ceremony or two]. . . .
>
> These apparently childish activities can be justified to a certain extent. The Nabis were predominantly intellectual and mystical in outlook; they felt as great a need to escape their bourgeois origins (except for Vuillard and Denis, all came from very respectable families) as to avoid the formulae of Impressionist and academic painting. Hence the creation of a world of their own. Some, like Sérusier were theosophists, read Maurice [sic] Schuré, and maintained contacts with the Rosicrucians. Maurice Denis was a practicing Christian.[72]

Denis's devout Catholicism did not prevent him from investigating Theosophy and Rosicrucianism and from being fascinated by them. However, such contacts were for him, as well as other Nabis, flirtations en route to a deepening of their Catholic faith.

As for Chausson, it would be interesting in the light of his erudition and broad culture to know what he thought of these movements that proved so attractive to his friends. That he was not only well aware of but also conversant with them we can be reasonably sure; in fact, his exposure to them could have been early, for his friend Odilon Redon, whom he had met in 1874 at Mme de Rayssac's salon, "had been initiated into Theosophical ideas" at that very place—"almost impossible to avoid for a man living in the intellectual milieus of Paris."[73] Edouard Schuré, whose esoteric book *The Great Initiates* profoundly influenced the Nabis "not less than the works of Maeterlinck,"[74] was a visitor to Bayreuth in 1883, as were Chausson, d'Indy, Duparc, and Lamoureux—the last a member of the Nabis. We can assume that Chausson's intellectual curiosity led him to read Schuré's work of 1889. Other sources of an esoteric kind with which Chausson could have had contacts were Villiers de l'Isle-Adam's drama *Axel,* in which "there is evidence that ceremonial magic and Rosicrucian initiation had been seriously pondered if not indulged in,"[75] and certainly some of Mallarmé's poetry. Indeed, it has been said that "Villiers de l'Isle-Adam introduced Mallarmé into various occult circles."[76]

Mallarmé himself speaks of the "Work" in five volumes that will take him twenty years to write.

> From this moment on [April 1866, a turning point not unlike a spiritual conversion], he had taken his position. For twenty years he worked in the shadows, cloistered within himself, spinning his web and elaborating what he would soon be calling "the Great Work, as our ancestors the alchemists used to say." For there was only one book to create, one which would reflect the structure and development of the universe and which would explain its hidden meaning through this reflection.
>
> It has been clearly established by now that if Mallarmé compared himself to an alchemist and his work to the Great Work, it was not merely a literary manner of speaking.[77]

In his authoritative book Michaud goes on to show how Mallarmé, more and more, "practiced hermeticism quite deliberately."[78] However, one of the most interesting aspects of this hermeticism was that it held itself aloof from "the noisy manifestations that were soon organized around these ideas, such as the famous Rosicrucian 'salon' at which a crowd amassed to hear Sar Péladan's prophecies. Mallarmé was always forearmed against hasty adventures of the mind."[79] This was in contrast with the well-publicized associations of Erik Satie with Péladan and the Rose + Croix Salon for which he composed music; Debussy was also involved in occult projects.[80] With respect to Chausson, there is no evidence at the moment that he was interested in these matters beyond general curiosity, but the potential for avid interest was certainly present in the friendship between him and Mallarmé, and it would have been a simple matter for him to have acquired hermetic knowledge from the poet. We can be sure, however, that Mallarmé's aloofness would have been characteristic of Chausson's own approach had there been a deep interest. If one is ever demonstrated, we are not likely to find that Chausson was a member of any of the occult societies; they would have been too sensational and flamboyant for his quiet tastes.

What we do know of Chausson's religious life ties in with the observations previously made concerning his generosity and self-effacement; both of these qualities are, in his own words, at the heart of the Gospel.[81] "Chausson believed more in the Christ of the Gospel, who embodied in his eyes an enduring model, than in the figure of the Saviour as presented by the successors of St. Peter."[82] An incident that undoubtedly bolstered this view occurred when, during one of his Italian sojourns, Chausson beheld Pope Leo XIII being carried in great pomp on his portable throne at St. Peter's. He also expressed his views on death in a poignant letter of 1894 to Henri Lerolle; the occasion was the death of his father. In the letter he voiced the belief that death is "the most positively real instant of our existence," that it is "not an end but a beginning or a re-beginning."[83]

No discussion of Chausson's life and character is complete without a detailed account of his relationships to two of the most important and influential composers on the French musical scene of his time—César Franck and Richard

Wagner. I begin with Franck, for he was the more immediate and visible of the two.

Chausson was one of the most important members of "la bande à Franck," that fiercely loyal group of pupils which revolved around the figure who had a major share in the regeneration of musical France after the military debacle of 1870-71—César Franck. The latter was a transitional figure in the sense that he bridged the gap between the period of operatic domination and the reemergence of France as a musical power based on traits that have always distinguished French music from the music of other nations. These characteristics need to be set forth here for the purpose of determining Franck's and his pupils' relationships to them. Donald Grout has provided us with a concise summary:

> The specifically French tradition is something essentially classical: it rests on a conception of music as sonorous form, in contrast to the Romantic conception of music as expression. Order and restraint are fundamental. Emotion or depiction are conveyed only as they have been entirely transmuted into music. That music may be anything from the simplest melody to the most subtle pattern of tones, rhythms, and colors; but it tends always to be lyric or dancelike rather than epic or dramatic, economical rather than profuse, simple rather than complex, reserved rather than grandiloquent; above all, it is not concerned with delivering a Message, whether about the fate of the cosmos or the state of the composer's soul.[84]

Martin Cooper says much the same in the following passage:

> to seek in French music primarily for a revelation of the composer's soul or for marks of the sublime is to look for something which the French consider a by-product.[85]

The current appraisal of Franck with respect to these French ideals is that he introduced foreign elements, specifically German, into his music with the result that he is not and cannot be called a typically French composer (ignoring for the moment that he was in actuality a Belgian). With reference to this point, G. Jean-Aubry asks:

> But is it French, this mysticism, this ignorance of irony, this taste for metaphysic, this readiness to take everything seriously, this need to prove something, this absence of critical sense, this imperviousness to the strong sensuousness of the Latins, and this taste in formal development in which can be found the characteristics of the Teutonic race?[86]

Franck's Germanic elements may be divided into two parts—the philosophical and moral outlooks and the musical traits that, most probably, were intended to express those convictions. With respect to the former, the conflict between Good and Evil is one of Franck's chief concepts. It is the subject of his symphonic poems, *Le Chasseur maudit* and *Les Djinns,* and of the oratorios, *Rédemption* and *Les Béatitudes.* Even in much of the nondescriptive, absolute music there appears to be a self-conscious striving toward the sublime—another expression of Franck's moral climate.

The musical characteristics that are essentially German are a rather thick texture; a tendency toward heavy orchestration; chromaticism; frequent modulation; the presence of polyphony or, as Paul Henry Lang says about Franck, "a sort of pseudo-polyphony in which parts disappear before their mission is fulfilled, and in which the excessive modulation through chromatic alteration creates the impression of linear movement,"[87] and finally, an emphasis on such German forms as the symphony, sonata, variations, and chamber music.

The mention of Franck's Germanic elements is not meant to imply that the purely sensuous characteristics usually found in French music are never present. Concerning this point Cooper says, in discussing the composer's symphonic poem, *Les Éolides:*

Here (and later in the Scherzo of the String Quartet) the composer is less earnest than usual, no longer in conscious search of the sublime but more freely sensuous, more lightly armed and graceful. The chromatic effects are used less as a means of heightening the emotion and more as a kind of cosmetic, which beautifies the surface of the music and gives it an ambiguity and elusiveness as charming as the fairies of Leconte de Lisle's verses.[88]

Later Cooper remarks that in a large proportion of Franck's music the sensuous elements "are again and again interrupted, often brusquely, as though they were connected in the composer's mind with the obscuring of the ideal, the disappearance of the cloud from the temple."[89]

One serious problem stemming from Franck's largely German viewpoint is the emotional climate in which his followers habitually dwelt. This climate was intensified into a kind of adoration as Franck's lofty idealism and selfless devotion to his art revealed themselves to his pupils. Their love and loyalty went so far as to lift Franck above the level of ordinary men to the point of conferring what almost amounted to sainthood upon him; titles like *le Père Franck* and *Pater Seraphicus* bear witness to this. In time, a master-disciple relationship was created, and the pupils closed ranks around Franck in efforts to protect him from hostile critics and an unsympathetic public. This attitude seemed to assume literal proportions at public premieres of Franck's works, when the pupils sat in immediately surrounding seats.

How did such a supercharged emotionalism come to be? According to Edward Burlingame Hill,

Franck's ascendancy over his pupils springs from the spiritual reaction exercised upon them through his character. He taught the moral obligations of the artist, the need for elevated standards, the consideration of quality rather than quantity in the students' tasks, emotional sincerity as an absolute prerequisite in all artistic expression, and above all faith as a primary ingredient. Moreover,

Franck steadily inculcated a disdain for immediate success, and a disregard of the public as a prerequisite for attaining durability in a work of art. But vital and constructive as were Franck's maxims for guidance in the artists' career, the fact that he bore out these principles in his own life made them the more compelling.[90]

Franck's principles were implemented by the conviction that the fugue, sonata, symphony, and variations were still capable of serving as the means of sincere, emotional expression. His precepts, coming at a time when opera and light salon music wholly dominated the French musical scene, endeared him to musicians of like inclinations. But Hill's observations should be emphasized: Franck's moral and spiritual attitudes joined together with his musical ideals to forge an unbreakable bond between him and his pupils. If to all these moral and musical standards be added Franck's uncomplaining acceptance of the almost continuous disappointments in his humdrum life, it will be apparent how much greater were the admiration and devotion of his pupils. As fame began slowly and belatedly to come to Franck, defense was followed by positive attempts to spread the gospel. The chief figure in this undertaking was Vincent d'Indy. With the death of Franck in 1890 he became the unquestioned leader of *la bande à Franck.*

Although in his biography of Franck d'Indy points out some of his teacher's musical failings, one receives the impression that he is apologetic about them. Thus, in discussing *Les Béatitudes* he explains away the weakness and theatricality of certain sections that are supposed to depict evil by saying that Franck's nature was too beautiful to be able to portray evil.[91] Analyses of Franck's music also appear in d'Indy's *Cours de composition musicale.*[92] Here, the enthusiasm sometimes gets out of hand, particularly where formal structures are discussed and d'Indy assigns Franck a place alongside Beethoven and Bach.

It is a strange paradox that d'Indy, the most intellectual member of the Franck circle and a man whose self-discipline was abundantly apparent, could have been so emotional on the subject of Franck. A possible explanation is that he was given to strong enthusiasms generally, and had a tendency to be very thorough in all his undertakings. Whatever the explanation, he is now credited with having created a legend that is hardly believable in toto.[93] Scattered here and there in earlier parts of his biography of Franck, Léon Vallas gives accounts of the strong, militant attitudes and behavior of the Franckists together with the ridicule and hostility they provoked. There is evidence that the pupils led and that Franck followed. This is apparent in a remark made by Charles Bordes, a member of the circle and one of the founders of the Schola Cantorum, when he said "Father Franck is the offspring of his pupils!"[94]

The emotional climate of the Franckists also expressed itself in some of their music. To cite an extreme example, Guillaume Lekeu, Franck's young Belgian pupil, described a projected movement of a work (which he did not live to complete) as embodying "the radiant development of Goodness."[95] This as well as other statements by Lekeu concerning the emotional content of his work represent, perhaps, the climax in the Franckists' emotional attitudes.

We may now examine some of the ways in which these emotionally exaggerated attitudes have been—and still are— a decided hindrance to objective analyses and evaluations of the music of the Franckists. The results of the overemotional defense and promulgation of Franck's spiritual and musical ideals can well be imagined. Not only did Franck's supporters do him "continuous harm by their sincere but exaggerated eulogies, by the excessive harshness they poured over those who were not among the devotees of the Société Nationale, and by their merciless condemnation of all who would not share their whole-hearted faith,"[96] but they incurred the wrath of those critics who had directed their fury against Franck. The unavoidable result, of course, was that the Franckists brought the same condemnation on their own heads and thus prevented a just assessment of their own music. How far this process went can be seen in a criticism of Chausson written by one Félicien Fagus in *Revue Franco-Allemande,* 1898. The author, after mentioning how "The Club Vincent d'Indy-Bréville-Chausson persists in punishing listeners with its student exercises," goes on to speak of the "Three Anabaptists entrenched at the Société Nationale behind their fortified and walled chapel"—the latter perhaps a sneering reference to Franck's former position at Ste Clothilde. The savage attack concludes with a reference to the drum made out of the hide of César Franck, "a drum on which Willy [the music critic Henri Gauthier-Villars] advertises their short-winded glory!"[97]

The use of the term *student* implies, of course, awkward imitations. That there are similarities between pupils and teacher cannot be denied, but the exact extent of them has seldom been indicated. It is perfectly possible for Franck's pupils to have applied their master's principles and methods in a personal and individual way; indeed, a study of much of their music shows that a number of them did just that. After all, one of Franck's basic admonishments was to be oneself without imitating anyone. But the critics saw no such distinction, their assumption being that the use of cyclical form in large works, for example, automatically meant slavish imitation of Franck's cyclical methods.

With regard to cyclical form, it is here that the essential truth of Bordes's statement that Franck "is the off-spring of his pupils" can be seen. In their enthusiasm the pupils magnified certain traits in their teacher's music and overemphasized those aspects which they especially wished to bring to the public's attention; this is particularly true with regard to cyclical form. Because the germs of this method of formal organization appear in Beethoven and because Franck knew Beethoven's later works wherein this method is used to advantage, the Franckists, d'Indy in particular, took great pains to demonstrate Franck's every use of the device. They undoubtedly found support in Franck's own statement concerning his Symphony in D minor: "the finale, just as in Beethoven's Ninth Symphony, recalls all the themes, but in my work they do not make their appearance as mere quotations. I have adopted another plan, and made each of them play an entirely new part in the music."[98] The Franckists were thus able to assert triumphantly that Franck was in the direct line of descent from Beethoven, and carried on where the latter had stopped. Franck had employed cyclical form in two important earlier works—the Quintet and the Sonata for Violin and Piano—and was later to issue a statement concerning his String Quartet that is similar to the one just quoted. Bordes's assertion—cited earlier—proved to be correct, for the Franckists wanted (perhaps even needed) to believe that their master was a great musical architect in the Beethoven tradition and, in a sense, willed it so. It was thus that d'Indy presented Franck to posterity in his *Cours de composition musicale.* But Franck cannot measure up to d'Indy's image of him, the inevitable result being a downgrading not only of Franck but also of many of his pupils for beating the drum too hard. Thus there is a certain justification in the reference to the drumbeating by Willy in Fagus's quoted attack. D'Indy suffered less than the other Franckists because of his position as undisputed leader of the group for, despite his over-zealous adherence to all things Franckian, his intellect, logic, scholarship, self-discipline, and sincerity earned him respect.

It seems undeniable that today's critics and historians have merely repeated the biases of the critics of the Franckists' era without attempting to reassess the work of Franck's pupils.[99] This is especially true of Chausson; the fact that he died before reaching full artistic maturity is no reason for the harsh and indefensible criticisms written as recently as 1956 and quoted below; each judgment appeared as a review of *Ernest Chausson* by Barricelli and Weinstein. In Eric Blom's review, there are these words about Chausson's music:

> His work, though noble and technically unexceptionable, is singularly flavorless in itself: one is aware only of a dash of Wagner and handfuls of Franckian seasoning not very effectively disguising a general insipidity. . . .
> It is difficult enough to keep Franck alive today, but when we do want that sort of music—as we occasionally want anything with a pronounced flavour of its own—we go to him, not to the pupils who watered down his idiom and are now among the great unwanted of music. . . . It is difficult to imagine anybody asking for Chausson's music now, in France or out of it. [100]

In his review, Harold Johnson tells us:

> Everywhere in Chausson's music we feel the heavy hands of Wagner and Franck. [101]

Far in the background of such reporting there are several generations of neglect stemming from circumstances that arose during the lifetimes of many of the Franckists—the various new movements in music that eclipsed these composers. Merely recalling Debussy, Ravel, and *Les Six* in France; Schoenberg and his followers; Stravinsky, Bartók, and many others is enough. They have all claimed greater interest and attention because of the very revolutionary nature of their music. Chausson is one of the notable casualties in this sequence of events, and the majority of his music lies buried not so much because it has been found wanting as because it is largely unknown.

The influence of Richard Wagner in France is a complex and involved affair. Affected by it were not only musicians but also the leading French literary circles, among whom were the Symbolists, and French artists such as Fantin-Latour and Odilon Redon, both of whose paintings on Wagnerian themes are well-known. [102] In view of the close ties among musicians, painters, and literary figures in the 1880s and 1890s in France, Wagner's influence operated on several interpenetrating levels, each of which meant different things to different circles. There is the purely musical influence, in which are included such matters as Wagnerian harmony and orchestration. Then there are Wagner's aesthetic principles as set forth in his *Oper und Drama* and *Gesamtkunstwerk.* Finally, there is the literary aspect of Wagner's own libretti, the philosophical ideas behind them, and the psychological and symbolic interpretations that can be assigned to them.

Emphasizing the nonmusical side of Wagner was *La Revue Wagnérienne,* founded in 1885 by Edouard Dujardin. It was published monthly for three years and presented Wagner in the roles of "poet, thinker, and creator of a new artform."[103] Among its contributors were Verlaine; Joris Karl Huysmans, author of the famous (or infamous) novel *À rebours;* Villiers de l'Isle-Adam; and Mallarmé. All of their contributions are illustrative of what came to be known as "literary Wagnerism;" Verlaine and Mallarmé, for example, each wrote a sonnet to Wagner. In time "Wagner acquired so many different interpretations, being endowed with a different significance for each of the conflicting symbolist groups, that after the third year of its publication *La Revue Wagnérienne* could no longer claim to represent Wagner's interests exclusively."[104]

Musical Wagnerism, however, was very real and was a result of direct contact with Wagner's music at Bayreuth. For years French musicians, literary figures, and artists had been making summer journeys thence in the reverent spirit of pilgrims going to a holy shrine. Among the composers were Saint-Saëns, Delibes (whose irreverent attitude scandalized d'Indy[105]), Dukas, Massenet, Chabrier, d'Indy, Lekeu, Duparc, Fauré, Chausson, and Debussy. The intensity of the Bayreuth atmosphere and, especially, the emotional impact of the music can be judged by the fact that in 1889 Lekeu fainted after the prelude to *Tristan* "and had to be carried out of the theatre."[106] Chabrier was equally emotional at a performance of the same work in Munich when, as d'Indy relates, "he burst into sobs of despair before even the first note of the Prelude. To his friends who enquired whether he was ill he could only reply, 'Oh that open A on the cello! Fifteen years I've been waiting to hear it!'"[107] Chausson was present at the 1882 and 1883 performances of *Parsifal;* in 1889 he was in Bayreuth again for *Tristan, Parsifal,* and *Meistersinger.* In addition to the Bayreuth performances French visitors also heard Wagner in Munich (Chausson's 1879 and 1880 visits have already been noted).

Because of the tremendous struggle that Chausson and other French composers experienced in the 1880s and 1890s in their efforts to throw off the Wagnerian musical yoke, it is appropriate to examine here Chausson's opinions of and attitudes toward Wagner. At first there is unreserved acceptance, as the following excerpt from a letter dated Munich, July 22, 1880, to Mme de Rayssac indicates:

> I have heard *Tristan,* which is marvelous; I don't know any other work which possesses such intenseness of feeling. As pure music it is splendid and of the highest order; as a way of understanding the musical drama it is a revolution.[108]

A little later we find Chausson expressing attitudes of doubt and frustration. In a letter of February 1883 to Mme de Rayssac he says, "and now Wagner is dead! But he has written *Tristan!*"[109] In another letter to her dated August 16, 1884, he assures her that he had done all he could "in order to avoid being too Wagnerian."[110] In a letter of the same year to Poujaud he speaks of "the red spector of Wagner that does not let go of me," and goes on to say, "I reach the point of detesting him. Then I look through his pages, trying to find hidden vices in him and I find them."[111] Again, in 1886 there are these remarks to Poujaud to whom the composer had sent the first sketches of his opera *Le Roi Arthus:*

> The greatest defect of my drama is without doubt the analogy of the subject with that of *Tristan.* That would still not matter, if I could only successfully de-Wagnerize myself. Wagnerian in subject and Wagnerian in music, is that not too much altogether?[112]

Finally, in another letter to Poujaud written in 1888, we find this sentence: "There is above all that frightful Wagner who is blocking all my paths."[113] All of these passages, of course, demonstrate a growing awareness of the dangerous consequences that could result from an uncritical acceptance and imitation of Wagner. As the body of Chausson's music reveals itself in subsequent pages, it remains to be seen how well or how poorly the composer heeded his own reservations.

One of the most fascinating chapters in Chausson's life is his relationship with Debussy, although certain areas of it are obscure. It is not clear, for example, just when the two composers first met one another. The first time their names are linked together publicly is the summer of 1889, when both of them were in Bayreuth. But there is evidence that they had known each other some months earlier, for Chausson had asked Debussy to submit his *Printemps* for a coming meeting of the Société Nationale. "The response of Debussy, dated 7 March, 1889, shows that a certain familiarity had already been established between them."[114] In 1890 Chausson and Étienne Dupin, a wealthy businessman, financed a limited and de luxe edition of Debussy's *Cinq Poèmes de Baudelaire.* And in 1891 Debussy dedicated his song *La Mer est plus belle* to Chausson; later, one of the *Proses lyriques*—"De fleurs"—was dedicated to Mme Chausson. It is, of course, entirely possible that the two men had met earlier than 1889, but until further evidence is available the matter must remain conjectural. As for the subsequent close friendship between them, conclusive evidence is provided by their correspondence dating from most of 1893 and the early part of 1894; the bulk of it appears in the issue of *Mercure de France* for December 1, 1934.[115]

There was a complete break between Chausson and Debussy—probably in 1894. In February of that year Debussy announced his formal engagement to Thérèse Roger, a singer and friend of the Chaussons. A month later it was mysteriously broken, which incurred Chausson's displeasure. These dates coincide with what appears to be the abrupt termination of the Chausson-Debussy correspondence, for after March 1894, there was silence. Lockspeiser cites a letter of May 15, 1959, from Mme Étiennette Lerolle-Chausson, the composer's then-living eldest daughter, in explanation of the rift: "Financial questions played a part in their estrangement, particularly as there appeared to be an element of double dealing. . . . My father was also very annoyed by the strange engagement, fortunately but very unpleasantly broken off, with our friend Thérèse Roger."[116]

In retrospect, it is surprising that Chausson and Debussy remained together for as long as they did. They were totally different in background, including "fortune, education, religion and a certain conception of life and of art. The one, without being in any way a conformist, remained attached to bourgeois conventions; the other was judged as a 'playboy' by his comrades."[117] This "playboy" had won the Prix de Rome in 1884, had served his required two years at the Villa Medici, and had returned to Paris in February of 1887; he was twenty-five years old and had not yet found himself artistically. In the background were the highly original keyboard improvisations and harmonic experiments during his student days at the Paris Conservatoire, a number of songs, and the works written in fulfillment of the requirements for the Prix de Rome. He needed money and introductions to influential circles where there were opportunities for material betterment. Chausson provided both soon after their probable 1889 meeting, having recognized Debussy's originality and future promise. Thus the early stages of the relationship suggest a subordinate role for Debussy that was not likely to change until he had attained some degree of artistic maturity. That Debussy accepted this role as late as 1893 is evident from a letter of August 26 to Chausson in which he writes:

> As for your sermons, they are always very dear to me; you are somewhat like a big, older brother in whom one has complete confidence and from whom one even accepts an occasional scolding; and forgive me if until now I have not succeeded in satisfying you, but rest assured nevertheless that any reproach from you would grieve me so much that it is impossible for me not to do all in my power so as never to deserve any.[118]

Again, under date of September 6 we read:

> And now the hour of my thirty-first year has struck, and I am still not very sure of my aesthetics, and there are things which I still do not know (how to write masterpieces, for example, and being very serious among other things, having the defect of dreaming away my life too much, and of seeing its realities only at the moment when they are becoming insurmountable). Perhaps I am more to be pitied than blamed; at any rate, in writing this I am counting on your pardon and your patience. . . .

LATEST NEWS

C. A. Debussy is completing a scene from *Pelléas et Mélisande,* "A fountain in the park" (Act IV, scene IV), on which he would like to have the opinion of E. Chausson.[119]

Lockspeiser confirms Debussy's uncertainty by remarking that "of the music he wrote during the five years following his return from Rome, he was satisfied with very little."[120]

Chausson, however, despite his wealth and position seems

to have been little better off for, in his reply to Debussy written perhaps the following day, we find these words:

> To be "very sure of one's aesthetics," good heavens, that is quite a job. You complain that you are not settled at the age of thirty-one. What am I going to say, being no longer thirty-one and torn by uncertainties, gropings in the dark and uneasiness?[121]

From this point on, however, the correspondence becomes more equalized as the friendship deepened. It is evident that the relationship meant a great deal to each of them, from both a personal and musical standpoint for, with respect to the latter, there are extended passages in the letters where suggestions and criticisms are offered regarding works being written by each. Gradually, as Debussy gained more confidence through experience and saw himself becoming established, if not always accepted, in musical circles, he grew bolder in his sharply perceptive advice to Chausson:

> I would like to have enough influence on you to be able to scold you and to tell you that you are fooling yourself! You exert so much pressure on your ideas that they no longer dare appear before you for fear of not being dressed up properly. You do not let yourself go enough and, above all, you do not give free reins to that mysterious thing which makes us find the impression of a feeling that is just right, when persistent and obstinate research is bound only to weaken it. I am so thoroughly convinced that you have within you all the desirable expression that I am pained when I see you enervate yourself in useless struggles. . . . Perhaps I don't have the right to speak to you this way, but forgive me and see in it only a great desire to see you what you should be and that as much as possible, because you are more capable of it than anybody. . . . I would simply like to give you courage to believe in yourself.[122]

The above remarks are, of course, merely further corroborations of the discussions above of the effects of the traits and habits that did much to weaken Chausson's music.

Although there appears to be no doubt of Debussy's sincerity in his feelings for Chausson, one cannot help wondering whether, in the light of the former's genius and fast-growing recognition, the relationship had not reached its peak. Certainly Chausson did not take offense at remarks like those just quoted; he was too honest not to realize their accuracy. But Debussy's star was clearly in the ascendancy, evidence of which is found in the last line of the letter from which the above passage was taken; there, Debussy makes reference to the coming festival of his music in Brussels on March 1; works played there were the String Quartet, about which Chausson had unexplained reservations that "grieved" Debussy very much; *La Damoiselle élue;* and two of the *Proses lyriques.* With time it seems clear that the relationship might have dissolved, or at least become less close because of the divergent musical paths on which each composer was embarked, to say nothing of the vast differences in temperament between them. It is the latter that seem to have caused the final rift shortly after the letter of February 1894. Debussy still needed financial help, and a scheme that was designed to benefit him involved a series of ten lecture-demonstrations he was to conduct on the music of Wagner at the home of Mme Escudier, Chausson's mother-in-law. Only five of the ten meetings ever took place, and Chausson, in a letter of March 19, 1894, to Henri Lerolle, speaks of having to return half of the subscription money.[123] This may have been the "element of double dealing" mentioned above by Mme Lerolle-Chausson. If no reasonable explanation was forthcoming from Debussy to account for his failure to complete the series—and there seems to have been none—one can only deplore his irresponsibility, a conclusion with which Chausson undoubtedly agreed. Coupled with this failure was the distressing affair involving Thérèse Roger. Thus it seems logical to conclude that Chausson was thoroughly disgusted and that, sooner or later, a separation was bound to occur based on two differing life-styles.

It is to Debussy's credit that he did not allow the rupture to prejudice his judgments concerning Chausson's music. In his role some years later as music critic for various Paris journals, Debussy pointed out what he considered to be his former friend's virtues as well as his shortcomings.[124] And at the time of Chausson's tragic death five years after the breach in their relationship, Debussy was among the mourners at the funeral.

NOTES

1. Jean-Pierre Barricelli and Leo Weinstein, *Ernest Chausson: The Composer's Life and Works* (Norman: University of Oklahoma Press, 1955), p. 6.

2. Anatole France, *La Vie littéraire* (Paris: Calmann-Levy, 1907), 2:105–14.

3. Jean Gallois, *Ernest Chausson: L'homme et son oeuvre* (Paris: Éditions Seghers, 1967), p. 7.

4. Roseline Bacou, "Décors d'appartements au temps des Nabis," *Art de France* 4 (Paris: Hermann, 1964):201.

5. Gustave Kahn, *Fantin-Latour* (Paris: F. Rieder & Cie., 1926), p. 47. The plaster in question appears to be that of the *Esclave* of Michelangelo rather than a Greek work of art.

6. Gallois, *Ernest Chausson,* p. 9.

7. Ibid., p. 21.

8. Quoted by Gaston Carraud in "Ernest Chausson," *Le Ménestrel* 82 (April 2, 1920):137–38.

9. Charles Oulmont, *Musique de l'amour* (Paris: Desclée de Brouwer & Cie., 1935), 1:95–96.

10. Mentioned by Maurice Denis in his *Journal: 1884–1904* (Paris: La Colombe, 1957), 1:225–26. An entry for "Pentecôte" 1897 mentions the colors to be employed for *Terrase de Fiesole,* 121.

11. Oulmont, *Musique de l'amour,* 1:141.

12. Jean-Paul Crespelle, *Les Maîtres de la belle époque* (Paris: Hachette, 1966), p. 25.

13. Princesse Edmond de Polignac, "Memoirs," *Horizon* 12, no. 68 (August 1945): 126.

14. Ibid., 127.

15. Reproduced on p. 115 of Stuart Preston, *Vuillard* (New York: Abrams, 1972).

16. Denis, *Journal,* 1:151.

17. Gallois, *Ernest Chausson,* p. 69.

18. Ibid.

19. Denis, *Journal,* 1:151.

20. Edward Lockspeiser, *Debussy: His Life and Mind* (London: Cassell, 1962), 1:126. There is no denying the doubt that has surrounded Chausson's death, for it seems inexplicable that such damage could have been inflicted unless the slope were long and steep (such doubts are certainly implied in the remarks of Gallois and Denis quoted above), but suicide does not appear to be the answer for a very practical reason: such a method had no guarantee as to its success. Failure would have meant a possibly permanent crippling of limbs and, at the very worst, head injuries that would have reduced Chausson to a vegetablelike existence. The suicidal theory also fails to take into account Chausson's personality, and his religious views on life and death—all of which will be explored presently and all of which appear to refute suicidal tendencies despite periods of gloomy self-doubt. Thus unless and until overwhelming evidence presents itself, Chausson's death must be regarded as a tragic accident.

21. Benoît's homage is reproduced in Gallois, *Ernest Chausson,* pp. 70–71.

22. Gustave Samazeuilh, "Ernest Chausson et le 'Roi Arthus,'" *La Revue Musicale,* December 15, 1903, 701.

23. Maurice Denis, *Henri Lerolle et ses amis* (Paris: 1932), p. 7.

24. Samazeuilh, "Ernest Chausson et le 'Roi Arthus,'" 705.

25. Ibid.

26. Ibid.

27. Quoted by Carraud in "Ernest Chausson," 137.

28. Princesse Edmond de Polignac, "Memoirs," 122.

29. First published by Enoch in 1897, Chausson's eulogy is reproduced by Francis Poulenc in *Emmanuel Chabrier* (Paris: La Palatine, 1961), pp. 133–34.

30. Barricelli and Weinstein, *Ernest Chausson,* p. 46.

31. Ibid., p. 33. Letter of June 1886 to Poujaud.

32. Ibid., pp. 38–39. Letter of 1888 to Poujaud.

33. Ibid., p. 44. Letter of 1889 to Poujaud.

34. Ibid., p. 46. Letter of 1890 to Poujaud.

35. Chausson's self-doubts with regard to Wagner's influence in France are by no means unique. Such lack of confidence was a major and universal problem among French composers of the period, as Elliott Zuckerman attests in his *The First Hundred Years of Wagner's Tristan* (New York: Columbia University Press, 1964).

36. Narrated by Carraud in "Ernest Chausson," 138. Of course, as Carraud remarks, Chausson's self-doubts had been strengthened by the infrequency with which his works were performed.

37. Ibid.

38. Gallois, *Ernest Chausson,* p. 43.

39. Quoted by Carraud in "Ernest Chausson," 138.

40. Arthur Symons, "A French Blake: Odilon Redon," *The Art Review* (July 1890).

41. Jacques Feschotte, Directeur de l'École Normale de Musique, relates in "Ernest Chausson et la poésie," *Musica* (Paris), September 1957, how Chaus-

son and Mallarmé became friends. It seems that Chausson mentioned to Maurice Bouchor (a poet and one of the composer's close friends) that he would like to learn English. Bouchor suggested lessons with Mallarmé, then retired in Paris on a very modest income. Chausson accepted enthusiastically. A number of notes (unpublished) bear witness to their friendship. One from Mallarmé, dated January 18, 1890, says: "Je suis, de loin, et depuis toujours, un de vos fervents. . . ." Later, Mallarmé expressed his gratitude for a concert invitation: "J'avais à vous remercier de m'avoir donné le contentement nouveau d'applaudir, puis d'ouïr le quatuor Ysaÿe."

Mallarmé was accustomed to addressing the envelopes of notes and letters to his friends in little four-line rhymes. These are all published in his *Oeuvres complètes* (Paris: Éditions Gallimard, 1965) under the general title of "Les Loisirs de la poste," and are grouped according to *écrivains, peintures,* and *musiciens.* Chausson's rhyme is no. 54 in the total series, and reads thus (p. 91):

> Arrête-toi, porteur, au son
> Gémi par les violoncelles,
> C'est chez Monsieur Ernest Chausson
> 22 Boulevard de Courcelles.

Mallarmé also appears to have been a frequent dinner guest at the Chaussons, as the following notes indicate: to Redon, "Come to dinner; you will find Lerolle, Rouart, without doubt Gide and Mallarmé." To Poujaud, the invitation mentions Lerolle, Bouchor, Degas, Redon, and Mallarmé.

42. See Anna Balakian, *The Symbolist Movement: A Critical Appraisal* (New York: Random House, 1967); C. M. Bowra, *The Heritage of Symbolism* (London: Macmillan & Co., Ltd., 1947); Guy Michaud, *Mallarmé,* trans. Marie Collins and Bertha Humez (New York: New York University Press, 1965); and Edmund Wilson, *Axel's Castle* (New York: Charles Scribner's Sons, 1932).

43. Camille Mauclair, *Le Soleil des morts: roman contemporain* (Paris: Paul Ollendorff, 1898). See Lockspeiser's *Debussy: His Life and Mind,* Appendix F, 1:223–28 for an excellent summary of this novel.

44. Gallois, *Ernest Chausson,* p. 79.

45. Bowra, *The Heritage of Symbolism,* p. 3.

46. Wilson, *Axel's Castle,* p. 20.

47. Quoted by Michaud in *Mallarmé,* pp. 15–16.

48. Bowra, *The Heritage of Symbolism,* p. 14.

49. Ibid., p. 13.

50. Balakian, *The Symbolist Movement,* p. 74.

51. In a letter to Raymond Bonheur, a close friend of both Chausson and Debussy, Chausson explains why he did not set Mallarmé: "Do you not know a modern poet who puts too many topazes in his verse?" It is impossible to translate *topazes* into anything but its English equivalent. The idea, however, seems unmistakably to imply the use of language that is rich and concentrated, too perfect and gemlike to serve as the basis for a musical setting, where concrete rather than abstract imagery is preferable.

52. Most of the points of view have been negative for, regardless of whether Chausson was setting Maeterlinck or composing in categories that have nothing to do with the *mélodie,* many of the adverse criticisms are the same: harmonies that are too "modern" and modulations that are too "abrupt." The question of the suitability of the harmonies for texts like those of Maeterlinck and others has hardly been raised, with the result that one reads statements like the following: ". . . and with his settings of Maeterlinck's *Serres chaudes* (1893–6) and *La chanson bien douce* [Verlaine] the atmosphere, like the texture, becomes unbearably thick and heavy—the 'unrelieved elegiac atmosphere', as one critic impatiently describes it." Martin Cooper, *French Music: From the Death of Berlioz to the Death of Fauré* (London: Oxford University Press, 1951), pp. 63–64.

53. Wilson, *Axel's Castle,* p. 257.

54. Balakian, *The Symbolist Movement,* pp. 80–81.

55. Georges Duthuit, "Vuillard and the Poets of Decadence," *Art News* 53, no. 1 (March 1954): p. 30.

56. Arthur Symons, *Dramatis Personae* (Indianapolis: Bobbs-Merrill, n.d.), p. 97.

57. Gallois, *Ernest Chausson,* p. 78.

58. Ibid., p. 79.

59. Ibid., p. 80.

60. Ibid., pp. 80–81. Letter of 1885 to Mme de Rayssac.

61. On page 29 of *Ernest Chausson,* Gallois raises the question of a possible unhappy love affair that, in his twenties, may have dictated Chausson's poetic choices. He singles out *Nanny* and *Le Charme* of Op. 2 as possible evidence for this theory.

62. Samazeuilh, "Ernest Chausson et le 'Roi Arthus,' " 705.

63. Gallois, *Ernest Chausson,* p. 76.

64. Ibid., p. 144. The close connection between Turgenev's *Le Chant de l'amour triomphant* and Chausson's *Poème* is pointed out here and on following pages; it appears later in the present volume in conjunction with the analysis of Chausson's work.

65. Quoted in Oulmont, *Musique de l'amour,* pp. 102–3.

66. The name was first applied by Henri Cazalis, sympathetic friend of the group, a doctor, and close friend of Mallarmé and Francis Jammes, the poet. He was also a minor Parnassian poet writing under the pseudonym of Jean Lahor; his *Sérénade* was set by Chausson (*Quatre Mélodies,* Op. 13, no. 2).

67. Denis, *Journal,* 1:135, 138.

68. Hans H. Hofstätter, *Geschichte der europäischen Jugendstilmalerei* (Köln: M. DuMont Schauberg, 1963), p. 86.

69. Jean-Paul Crespelle, *The Fauves* (Greenwich: New York Graphic Society, 1962), p. 40.

70. Agnès Humbert, *Les Nabis et leur époque* (Geneva: Pierre Cailler, 1954), p. 15.

71. Ibid., p. 44.

72. Crespelle, *The Fauves,* pp. 39–40.

73. Sven Sandström, *Le Monde imaginaire d'Odilon Redon* (Lund: 1955), p. 122.

74. G. Charensol, "Les Nabis," *Revue des Deux Mondes* (July, August 1955), 137.

75. John Senior, *The Way Down and Out: The Occult in Symbolist Literature* (Ithaca: Cornell University Press, 1959), p. 129. A concise summary of *Axel* is presented on pp. 129–33.

76. Paul Zweig, *The Heresy of Self-Love* (New York: Basic Books, Inc., 1968), p. 218. However, in spite of his Breton origin, which included an inherent interest in the occult, Villiers de l'Isle-Adam was an uncompromising Catholic.

77. Michaud, *Mallarmé*, pp. 64–65.

78. Ibid., p. 103.

79. Ibid., p. 129.

80. See pp. 21–31, "The Rosicrucian Adventure" in Rollo Myers, *Erik Satie* (New York: Dover Publications, Inc., 1968), and Appendix E, "Debussy and Occultism" in Lockspeiser, *Debussy: His Life and Mind*, 2:272–77.

81. Gallois, *Ernest Chausson*, p. 74.

82. Ibid.

83. Ibid., pp. 53–54.

84. Donald Jay Grout, *A History of Western Music*, rev. ed. (New York: W. W. Norton and Co., Inc., 1973), p. 650.

85. Cooper, *French Music*, p. 1.

86. G. Jean-Aubry, *French Music of Today*, trans. Edwin Evans (London: Kegan Paul, Trench, Trubner & Co., Ltd., 1926), p. 28.

87. Paul Henry Lang, *Music in Western Civilization* (New York: W. W. Norton and Co., Inc., 1941), p. 927.

88. Cooper, *French Music*, p. 30.

89. Ibid., p. 31.

90. Edward Burlingame Hill, *Modern French Music* (Boston: Houghton Mifflin Co., 1924), pp. 35–36.

91. Vincent d'Indy, *César Franck*, trans. Rosa Newmarch (London: The Bodley Head, Ltd., 1909), p. 55.

92. Vincent d'Indy, *Cours de composition musicale*, 3 vols. (Paris: Durand et Cie., 1950). Three specific Franck works analyzed by d'Indy are: Violin and Piano Sonata, 2, 1:423–26; String Quartet, 2, 2:259–66; Symphony in D minor, 2, 2:159–66. The reader is also referred to d'Indy's article on Franck's chamber music in Cobbett's *Cyclopedic Survey of Chamber Music*, comp. and ed. Walter Willson Cobbett, 2d ed. (London: Oxford University Press, 1963), 1:418–29.

93. For a discussion of the Franck legend and d'Indy's part in innocently creating it, the reader is referred to Norman Demuth, *César Franck* (London: Dennis Dobson, Ltd., 1949), pp. 205–8. On p. 205 there is a first-hand description by Guy Ropartz of Franck as he really was. Ropartz was one of the two surviving Franck pupils at the time Demuth's book was written, the second being Pierre de Bréville; in exploding the legend, Demuth consulted both of them.

94. Quoted in Léon Vallas, *César Franck*, trans. Hubert Foss (New York: Oxford University Press, 1951), p. 194.

95. Quoted in Cooper, *French Music*, p. 62. Here Cooper cites a trio as the work whose last movement was thus planned. However, on p. 70 another reference to

the movement states that it was intended for the Piano Quartet. This second reference appears to be the correct one for, on p. 67, Cooper lists the Piano Trio (one of a number of projected works in this form) as complete (it was finished in 1891), while the Piano Quartet is listed as incomplete. The deciding factor is Cooper's statement on p. 70 that Lekeu did not live to write the movement. An excellent discussion of Lekeu and his music appears in Laurence Davies, *César Franck and His Circle* (Boston: Houghton Mifflin Co., 1970), pp. 258–71.

96. Vallas, *César Franck*, p. 204.

97. Quoted in Gallois, *Ernest Chausson*, pp. 179–80.

98. Quoted in Vallas, *César Franck*, p. 213.

99. A notable exception that redresses this wrong is Davies's *César Franck and His Circle* (cited in n. 95). In this excellent work the music of teacher and pupils is discussed and evaluated, with relation to each other and to the historical and social environments in which they all lived and worked. One is especially impressed with the attention given to such relatively little known figures as Lekeu, Bordes, Castillon, Holmès, Magnard, and so on.

100. Eric Blom, Review of *Ernest Chausson: The Composer's Life and Works* (Barricelli and Weinstein), *Music and Letters* 37 (April 1956): 177.

101. Harold E. Johnson, Review of *Ernest Chausson: The Composer's Life and Works* (Barricelli and Weinstein), *Music Library Association Notes,* 2d ser. 13, no. 3 (June 1956):440.

102. The *Catalogue de l'oeuvre complet de Fantin-Latour* (Amsterdam-New York: B. M. Israel & Da Capo Press, 1969) lists between seventy-five and one hundred works (paintings, lithographs, drawings and sketches) portraying scenes from *Rienzi, Tannhäuser, Lohengrin, The Ring, Tristan, Meistersinger,* and *Parsifal.* Redon's work in this area constitutes a tiny fraction in comparison—less than a dozen works.

Evidence of Wagner's impact on the French literary world is apparent in the following studies: E. Carcassonne, "Wagner et Mallarmé," *Revue de Littérature Comparée* 16, no. 2 (April-June 1936):347–66.; E. Drougard, "Richard Wagner et Villiers de l'Isle-Adam," *Revue de Littérature Comparée* 14 (1934): 297–300., M. G. Wooley, *Richard Wagner et la symbolisme français* (Paris: Presses Universitaires, 1931). These titles represent but a small fraction of the total number that deal with this important subject.

103. Quoted in Cooper, *French Music*, p. 57.

104. Lockspeiser, *Debussy: His Life and Mind,* 1:101–2.

105. Ibid., p. 92 n.

106. From an article by Paul Landormy, an excerpt from which is printed in Léon Vallas, *Claude Debussy,* trans. Maire and Grace O'Brien (London: Oxford University Press, 1933), p. 76.

107. Quoted in Lockspeiser, *Debussy: His Life and Mind,* 1:95 n.

108. Quoted in Barricelli and Weinstein, *Ernest Chausson,* p. 11.

109. Ibid., p. 27.

110. Ibid.

111. Ibid., pp. 27–28.

112. Ibid., p. 72.

113. Ibid., p. 38.

114. François Lesure, "Claude Debussy, Ernest Chausson et Henri Lerolle," *Humanisme actif* (Paris: 1968), pp. 337–38.

115. Charles Oulmont, "Deux amis, Claude Debussy et Ernest Chausson," *Mercure de France* 256 (December 1, 1934):248–69.

116. Quoted in Lockspeiser, *Debussy: His Life and Mind,* 1:126 n. Chausson's complete bewilderment regarding the events surrounding this engagement appears in letters to Henri Lerolle (April 1894) printed in Lesure, "Claude Debussy, Ernest Chausson et Henri Lerolle," pp. 342–43.

117. Lesure, "Claude Debussy, Ernest Chausson et Henri Lerolle," p. 338. Chausson's middle-class conservatism is apparent in his refusal to ever permit Gabrielle Dupont ("Gaby"), Debussy's mistress, to enter his home. This statement by Lesure (p. 338) is in direct contradiction to an assertion by Victor Seroff in *Debussy; Musician of France* (New York: G. P. Putnam's Sons, 1956), p. 154. There Seroff remarks that after Gaby shot herself in 1897 upon discovering that Debussy was conducting an affair with another woman, she took refuge with Mme Chausson after leaving the hospital and "later on, at Madame Chausson's suggestion of 'a little change of surroundings,' Gaby went for a visit with the Ysaÿes in Brussels. Debussy said nothing at the time. But because of what he considered 'taking Gaby's side,' he cut off his relationship with his two dearest friends and their families."

118. Quoted in Barricelli and Weinstein, *Ernest Chausson,* p. 64.

119. Ibid.

120. Edward Lockspeiser, *Debussy* (New York: Pellegrini and Cudahy Inc., 1949), p. 51.

121. Quoted in Barricelli and Weinstein, *Ernest Chausson,* p. 65.

122. Ibid., pp. 68–69. From a letter probably written in February 1894.

123. Lesure, "Claude Debussy, Ernest Chausson et Henri Lerolle," p. 342.

124. The complete criticisms—all very brief—are contained in Léon Vallas, *The Theories of Claude Debussy,* trans. Maire O'Brien (London: Oxford University Press, 1929), pp. 46–48. The publications in which these comments appeared, together with the dates, are shown on pp. 182, 183, and 185 of Vallas's book.

2

The Mélodies

C HAUSSON'S *mélodies,* from *Les Lilas* of 1877 through *Chanson Perpétuelle* of 1898, span the entire creative period of their composer's life, except for a five-year hiatus in the middle, and are more numerous than the works in any other category—facts that suggest a natural affinity on Chausson's part for this peculiarly French genre.

Altogether there are thirty-five published *mélodies* for voice and piano as follows: Op. 2, seven; Op. 8, four; Op. 13, four; Op. 14, one; Op. 17, two; Op. 24, five; Op. 27, three; Op. 28, three; Op. 34, two; Op. 36, two; and two without opus numbers. For voice and orchestra there are two *mélodies* comprising the *Poème de l'amour et de la mer* (separated by an orchestral interlude), Op. 19; and *Chanson Perpétuelle,* Op. 37. Thus there are thirty-eight published *mélodies.* Remaining unpublished and without opus number are six more songs for voice and piano, making forty-one for this category and bringing the total of all *mélodies* to forty-four. Complicating the picture somewhat is the fact that the second of the two *mélodies* of *Poème de l'amour et de la mer* has been published separately with piano accompaniment as *Le Temps des lilas*—a circumstance that has made this fine song more accessible and easily the best known and best loved of all Chausson's *mélodies.*

The individual *mélodies* within opus numbers are often out of order with respect to their dates of completion. Such time lapses range from as little as a few days (Op. 2 where the date for *Nanny,* the first of the seven, is June 18, 1880, while that for the third, *Les Papillons,* is June 6) to several years (Op. 24 whose first *mélodie, Serre chaude,* was completed in 1896, while the second, *Serre d'ennui,* was written in 1893). It is more than likely that Chausson changed the order in the interests of unity when final decisions were made concerning the contents of an opus.

For a more complete understanding of Chausson's very real contribution to the literature of the song, it is essential that the word *mélodie,* as used here and subsequently, be defined and contrasted with its immediate French predecessor, the *romance.* In the chapter on French song in *A History of Song,* David Cox defines the *mélodie* in the following terms:

> From about the time of Berlioz the term *mélodie* has been used to signify the French *pièce vocale* (piece for the voice), with its combination of rhythmic flexibility, melodic subtlety, and harmonic richness, as we find on such a high level of perfection in the mature songs of such composers as Fauré, Duparc and Debussy. It is thus distinguished from the songs in which melodic line is everything.[1]

A more exact characteristic of the *mélodie* is mentioned by Sydney Northcote: "with Fauré and Duparc a new subtlety comes into the question of vocal declamation and it is not too much to say that this is one of the fundamental factors which determine the absolute identity of the *mélodie.*" Prior to this he had called attention to "the absence of real stresses in the French language. While this may indicate that the rhythm in French poetry must therefore be a matter of 'quantity' and not of periodic accent it also poses a peculiar problem in the matter of vocal declamation, especially when the words are set to music. For it then involves a subtlety in musical phrasing which no other European language demands."[2] Northcote observes that "the birth of the *mélodie* must always be associated with the Parnassien group of

French poets."[3] Although the word *mélodie* was in use from the time of Berlioz, it seems to have acquired significance as a separate genre only when composers began to set the poems not only of the Parnassians but also of the Symbolists. According to Northcote,

> the Parnassiens were a "school" of poets writing between the years 1866 and 1876. . . . They believed in impersonality; in the refinement and polish of work, phrase, rhythm and stanza; in a jewel-like hardness and clarity and vivid colour; and in general, they were far more concerned with perfection of form than with pure feeling or emotion. Besides, they were essentially miniaturists. In short, their ideals were sculptural, with a passion for ancient Greece and, often enough, a colourful orientalism. Their chief abhorrence was any form of vague rhapsodizing.[4]

Symbolism, on the other hand, is the counterpart of Impressionism in painting and music. There are the same vagueness of outline and the same pleasure in sensuous sound as are achieved in poetry by a careful selection of vowels and consonants; there is also the use of verbal symbols that themselves are sometimes intentionally obscure so as to represent things that are shadowy and ill-defined. However, common to both the Parnassians and Symbolists was a strong neopagan and hedonistic current that was perhaps not so much anti-Christian as it was non-Christian. One need only read Mallarmé's *L'Après-midi d'un faune* with its evocation of classical Greece to be aware of these currents. There is, of course, much more in the poetry of these schools than pastoral atmospheres, because ennui, irony, and resignation—all expressed as fleeting moods in miniature forms—are often present.

The *mélodies* that resulted when composers set the texts of the Parnassian and Symbolist poets have one point in common: they attempt to reproduce the moods of the poems as faithfully as possible insofar as music is capable. Thus the text is the point of departure, and it not only determines the form of the *mélodie* but also suggests by its nuances the choice of melodic contour, the harmony, and the rhythm, the last largely following that of the words. This is exactly the opposite procedure from that followed in the *romance,* where the words are made to conform to the predetermined factors of strophic form and the *phrase carrée* or "square phrase"—that is, the regular phrase of specified length that recurs with monotonous regularity throughout the song.

Frits Noske in his admirable study of the *mélodie*[5] mentions both strophic form and the *phrase carrée* as dominant traits of the *romance.* He includes an example from Méhul (a composer for whom Franck had a strong admiration) in which the prosody is correct at a certain point in the first stanza but incorrect at the corresponding place in the second. This condition is caused by the rigidity of the *phrase carrée,* which does not alter its length, note values, or pitches. Two further characteristics of the *romance* are a generally diatonic vocal line restricted to simple melodic contours, and a simple supporting harmony composed of block or arpeggiated chords.

The poems to which the majority of *romances* were set are by Romantic poets. These are often rhapsodic, atmospheric, and personal—qualities associated with Romanticism. Most of them do not contain the precise imagery that is one of the characteristics of the later poems associated with the *mélodie.* Many of their lines are of the same length and form *phrases carrées* when they are set to music, the ends of phrases nearly always coinciding with the punctuation at the ends of lines.

In contrast to this situation, in which defective prosody is almost certain, correct prosody is virtually assured when careful attention is paid to molding the entire *mélodie* around every nuance of the text. How carefully these nuances were observed is indicated by Bainbridge Crist when he shows how Debussy in his *mélodie C'est l'Extase langoureuse* set the words "C'est la nôtre, n'est-ce pas?"

A lesser artist than Debussy would have failed to see that "n'est-ce pas?" was asked after "C'est la nôtre" because of a lurking fear that disturbed the mind of the questioner. Debussy brings out this timorousness by employing a rest in the first half of beat 1, thereby necessitating a rapid approach of *n'est-ce* to the final word *pas.* ... If one will substitute two sixteenth notes for the triplet one will discover how completely the alteration destroys Debussy's exquisite effect.[6]

Fig. 1. Debussy; *C'est l'Extase langoureuse,* mm. 40–41

Many other examples could be cited, not only in Debussy but also in Duparc and Fauré, of a similar awareness of the psychological implications of a text. What sometimes appears to be defective prosody in some of their *mélodies*—the rhythmic prominence of conjunctions like *mais* and *et*—is really a demonstration of their profound understanding of the inner, subtle meanings of their texts. Whenever such prosody occurs in Franck or in other composers whose songs are similar to the *romance,* it is caused by the restrictions of the strophic form and the *phrase carrée.* However, the *mélodie* and strophic form are not mutually exclusive, for Duparc's *L'Invitation au voyage* and *Extase,* as well as some of Fauré's songs, are strophic. The difference between the strophic treatment in the *mélodie* and that of the *romance* is that in the former the succeeding stanza is altered melodically and harmonically (if necessary) to fit the textual requirements. This procedure is applied to the final stanza of Franck's *Nocturne* and in this respect the song approaches the *mélodie*. However, the regular phrase structure throughout the song and the strictness of the strophic form in the earlier stanzas, despite the rhythmic variations in the accompaniment and a few alterations in the vocal line to accommodate the text, are traits of the *romance*. Most if not all of the musical differences between the *romance* and the *mélodie* stem from the opposite concepts that govern each genre. In the *romance* the text merely served as a framework for the music; in the *mélodie* it gave birth to the music.

Considering the short history of the *mélodie* as a distinctive art form, an interesting question arises as to which *mélodies* by whom could have served as models for Chausson. Certainly not César Franck, whose total output of twenty-two songs must be regarded as of minor importance when compared with his instrumental and choral works. Indicative of their minor position is the fact that even Franck's staunchest supporters devote but scant space to any discussion of them. D'Indy mentions *Nocturne* and *La Procession,* two of Franck's mature songs, in one sentence in *Cours de composition musicale,* and excludes the songs entirely in his biography except for listing their titles and dates of composition. Vallas's reference to them in his biography is confined to dates of composition and performance; Demuth and van den Borren summarize them in a chapter each; and they are treated in a small section of Noske's study.

Five traits common to many of Franck's songs are their strophic settings; short phrases of two, three, or four measures repeated rhythmically; accompaniments consisting of chords either in block, broken, or arpeggiated form; extremely simple vocal lines; and at times a glaring disregard for correct text accentuation—all characteristics of the *romance*. Franck's disregard for correct accentuation is

pointed out by Noske at the very beginning of his discussion
of Franck's songs:

> Although he set the verse of some famous poets (e.g.,
> Hugo, Musset, and Sully-Prudhomme), it almost appears
> as if he chose them by chance, since he showed little re-
> spect for the rhythm of their lines. A section of "Ninon"
> (Musset), for example, is prosodized in this way:
> Ninon! Ninon! que fais-tu DE la vie? L'heu-RE s'enfuit,
> le jour succède au jour. Ro-SE ce soir, demain flétrie,
> Comment vis-tu, toi qui n'as pas d'amour?[7]

Poor text accentuation can be found also in Franck songs of
the 1870s, thirty years after the *Ninon* example (1842–43).
Several illustrations of it appear in *Lied* (1873) where the $\frac{6}{8}$
meter with the characteristic patterns ♪ | ♩ ♪ | ♪ |
and ♩. ♩ ♪ emphasizes the deficiency. Franck has placed
unimportant words like *à*, *comme, sur,* and *sous* on accented
quarters and dotted quarters at the beginnings of measures.
In considering this and other, later songs where defective
prosody is found, one is forced to conclude that it is not a
matter of youthful ineptness carried over into later songs but
rather that Franck was bent on carrying out a previously
determined and inflexible musical design without regard
for textual necessities. This observation is voiced in part by
Noske when, in speaking of the eight songs written between
1840 and 1850, he criticizes their weak structure by noting
that "the over-schematic forms do not issue from the musical thought but seem to have been fixed in advance."[8]

The four songs of Franck's maturity are *Le Vase brisé*
(1879), *Nocturne* (1884), *La Procession* (1888), and *Les
Cloches du soir* (1889). Of these, the second and third are
generally considered to be the finest, while opinions concerning the two others are somewhat negative. Each of the
four is too radically different from Chausson's songs to have
had even the slightest effect on the latter. Chausson's non-
use of strophic form left him completely free to delineate

the basic imagery of his texts as well as to interpret their subtleties, while Franck's dependence upon that form, coupled with his choice of poems whose romanticism is vague and imprecise, made such an approach impossible. Thus Franck is much closer in spirit and style to the *romance* than to the *mélodie*.

If, indeed, there had been any model to whom Chausson could have looked for guidance in *mélodie* composition, it would most likely have been Massenet. Because he was known primarily as an opera composer, it is often forgotten that he composed about 260 songs—more than any other French composer. While admitting that "Massenet's *mélodie* is so indissolubly linked to the now-vanished *fin-de-siècle* salon ambiance that its revival is highly unlikely," Noske mentions his skilled craftsmanship and credits him "with having finally delivered the *mélodie* from the yoke of the square phrase [*phrase carrée*]. He sacrifices the line as a structural element to the poetic content and introduces into the genre a sort of musical prose, capable of conveying all the nuances of the literary text. Of course the periodic phrase does not vanish completely. . . . In general, however, Massenet's *mélodie* tends toward the 'poem in prose,' more or less analogous to the free verse written by poets of the period."[9]

In like manner, Chausson's phrase structure, melodic lines, and rhythms are bound up together and operate as a unit because they proceed from the text that occupies him at the moment. A good illustration of this entire procedure is afforded by *Nanny,* the first *mélodie* of Op. 2. The poem, from Leconte de Lisle's *Poèmes antiques,* is a typical example of the Parnassian school; couched in precise imagery, its subject is a lost love. The poignant grief of the poem, expressed by the command that the forest, foliage, spring paths, heather, and so on are to weep, is admirably matched in the setting. Chausson begins his vocal line high and lets it descend through an octave, largely chromatically. Halfway through this first phrase, *pleurez* is set off by rests from the first part; the rests emphasize the poignancy of the chromatic setting by isolating the word from the previous chromaticism. In the second phrase, Chausson emphasizes the pathos still more by allowing the line to ascend a half-step higher before its descent, and by setting *pleurez* higher and preceding it with a long note from which it grows. These procedures create a sense of urgency, which is heightened by the increase in the phrase length from four to eight measures. The longer phrase results in a steady, downward pull to *et d'églantiers.* Also contributing to the tension are the sixteenth notes on *et* (before *toi* and *vous*).

Another example in *Nanny* of Chausson's care in the business of text-setting is his treatment of the French *e muet* or mute *e* at the ends of words. French composers invariably treat such words as though they were duo-or multisyllabic, the reason being to assure a rhythmic flow and a more liquid connection between words. To set these syllables to upward-moving leaps would be to distort them by giving undue emphasis, thus forcing a word like *rêve* into the impossible pattern of *rêVE.* The usual manner of treating such words is either to set the final syllable to the same note as that occupied by the preceding syllable or to allow it to fall stepwise or by leap. Chausson employed these methods in *Nanny* when he set *feuillages, source, vive, bruyères,* and *sauvages* (Fig. 2).

Occasionally the *e muet* is resolved upwards in a stepwise manner. When this occurs, the word containing the syllable is often found near the beginning or middle of a normally rising and falling melodic line, and no false accentuations exist because the word is absorbed into the line. The words *lune* and *chaque* in *Apaisement,* the first of Chausson's three Verlaine settings, illustrate this. Much more rarely, the situation just described occurs at a phrase ending; yet even here the stepwise progression does not seem to cause the *e muet* to be unduly stressed. An example may be found in *Le*

Fig. 2. Chausson; *Nanny,* mm. 1–14

Charme, Op. 2, no. 2, where, in measure 20, the word *charme* is set to quarter notes on F and G.[10]

The accompaniment to *Nanny* is of the flowing type whose broken figurations, thoroughly pianistic, encourage a forward, fluid movement that enhances the imagery of such words as *pleurez.*

Occasionally, the short and regularly recurring phrases so often found in Franck's songs occur in some of Chausson's *mélodies.* In such instances, however, it is not a Franckian influence that determines their usage but the poem that is being set. Some poems as they appear in print show lines of varying lengths, while others have lines of the same length. It is these latter that often produce *mélodies* whose phrases correspond to a line of poetry and are thus all equal in length. A *mélodie* of this type is *Le Charme,* the second member of the *Sept Mélodies* (Op. 2). Here, the commas at the ends of the lines coincide exactly with the endings of the musical phrases. This *mélodie* of only twenty-eight measures is perhaps Chausson's most concise, and its simplicity is almost Schubertian. Except for the concluding three measures, the top line of the accompaniment follows the vocal line faithfully, a rarity in Chausson's *mélodies.*

Les Papillons, third of the set, employs a poem by Théophile Gautier, one of the transitional figures between Romanticism and the Parnassian movement. It is a through-composed *mélodie,* as distinguished from the irregular ternary form of *Nanny* and the irregular two-part form of *Le Charme.* Except for *La Cigale* of Op. 13, it is the liveliest and most carefree of all Chausson's *mélodies.* Marked *vif,* its perpetual motion accompaniment is arrested for only three measures just before the concluding piano postlude quietly resumes the headlong pace. The sixteenth-note accompaniment is marked *pianissimo* throughout most of its murmurous course, one that sets the stage for Gautier's silent butterflies. There is a tinge of melancholy, however, as the poet asks whether the butterflies "would lend him their wings" so that he might go to his love and die. The mood of Chausson's setting is light, and a certain irony communicates itself to the listener, as if to shy away from any real sadness.

With *La Dernière Feuille,* also by Gautier, we are back in the world of lost loves and dreams, symbolized by autumn's last leaf and bird. Unlike the majority of Chausson's accompaniments, this one is largely chordal; its gently rocking motion coupled with the generally low tessitura of the vocal line creates a restless atmosphere that mirrors the desolation of the scene. One short passage near the end contains a virtually static rhythm and a one-note vocal line to underscore the lifeless lines, "love is waning, for winter is here." Earlier, in measures 19–20, a juxtaposition of major-minor modes occurs—a procedure much in evidence in both Schubert and Franck.

One final nuance that this writer feels would have improved the imagery concerns the very end. Here, under the line *"quand l'arbre sera vert"* ("when the tree will be green"), Chausson rocks back and forth over a tonic pedal point between a B-minor triad and a diminished seventh chord, coming to a final B-minor resting place under *vert.* A B-major chord under this word would have suggested a quiet, hopeful anticipation of the far-distant spring.

After the somber tone of *La Dernière Feuille,* the serene fifth *mélodie* of Op. 2, *Sérénade italienne,* comes as a welcome relief. Noticeable here is an increasing responsiveness of the vocal line to the rhythms of the poetry. In each of the *mélodies* thus far considered there has been a tendency in this direction, suggesting that Chausson was aware of the problems peculiar to the correct setting of French texts. Because French is a language without the heavier accentuation of English, German, and Italian, its syllables receiving nearly equal stress, a *parlando* style less frequently used in these languages results when a French poem is carefully set. Such a style need not necessarily be rapid or degenerate to a patter of words and notes in order to be recognizable as *parlando.* Passages containing even eighths and others employing even quarters—both signifying the even accents of French—abound in the *mélodies* just discussed. Frequently, passages of this type are separated by more conventional yet quite correct examples of prosody. The triplet groupings in the vocal line—so often seen in Debussy's *mélodies* as well as throughout *Pelléas et Mélisande*—also make their first appearances in these early *mélodies,* but it is in

Sérénade italienne that the first examples of *successive* triplets appear. However, two incorrectly set syllables stand out from the otherwise admirable prosody: *conDUIsent* (measure 16) and *DIsent* (measure 20).

Sérénade italienne is one of Chausson's most beautiful songs as well as one of the most spontaneous. Its flowing triplet figures and smooth vocal line are well suited to Paul Bourget's poem depicting a small boat on the sea, navigated by an old fisherman and his two sons who will not understand the words of love exchanged in the boat. Bourget was one of Debussy's poets, although he eventually gave way to Verlaine as that composer's knowledge and appreciation of current literature deepened.

Hébé, the sixth *mélodie* of Op. 2, is subtitled "Chanson grecque dans le mode phrygien," possibly as an act of homage to its dedicatee, Mlle Eva Callimaki-Catargi, the first half of whose name is startlingly like Callimachus, the Greek poet of the third century B.C. We may certainly infer that she was either Greek or of Greek descent for, as noted earlier, Fantin-Latour, a member of Mme de Rayssac's salon, painted her in the act of copying a Greek plaster. And, of course, the subject of the poem derives from Greek mythology.

From all of the above, it is not surprising that the mode chosen for this setting is not the ecclesiastical Phrygian (or third mode) but the ancient Greek Phrygian. At first glance the mode appears to be ecclesiastical Dorian (first mode),[11] because a great deal of the song centers around that mode's dominant—A—while the final cadence is on D and there are no accidentals of any kind. If, however, the mode were transposed, church Phrygian accidentals would have to be used. Therefore, assuming that Chausson knew the difference between Dorian and Phrygian when he gave the *mélodie* its subtitle, we are forced to consider the ancient Phrygian as the only alternative; when its notes (f-sharp to f-sharp) are placed within the so-called *characteristic octave* (e to e) and transposed down one tone, no accidentals occur, thus giving *Hébé* a church Dorian appearance as well as sound. In reality it is Greek Phrygian, a fact that once more demonstrates Chausson's erudition and discrimination in the sense of appropriateness for his dedicatee. As for the music itself, it is very simple; the accompaniment most of the time faithfully adheres to the vocal line. The total effect is one of innocence and charming naiveté.

The seventh and final *mélodie* of Op. 2, *Le Colibri (The Humming Bird),* to the poem of Leconte de Lisle, is noteworthy for its employment of $\frac{5}{4}$ meter throughout the song. Within this rather unusual framework, Chausson has written another charming song that unfolds in an effortless kind of way. In the middle there are some descending chromatic passages whose expressiveness suggests *Tristan,* but there is a quick return to the lightness and airiness with which the majority of the song is concerned.

Chausson's next collection of songs is that of Op. 8—*Quatre Mélodies sur des poèmes de Maurice Bouchor;* these range in date from 1882 to 1890. It is generally recognized today that Bouchor's poetry, a great deal of it concerned with the sentimental images of lost loves, is dated. One cannot but agree with Gallois that the close friendship of Chausson and Bouchor (they were exact contemporaries and studied law together) was responsible for the relatively large number of the latter's poems—fifteen including translations from Shakespeare, but not including the text for Bouchor's drama, *La Légende de Sainte Cécile*—that found their way into Chausson's *mélodies.* That the composer was aware of the inferior quality of his friend's poetry seems apparent in several of his settings, where his efforts are clearly superior to and transcend the faded and exaggerated emotions of the texts. This is especially true in *Poème de l'amour et de la mer,* one of Chausson's longer and more important works.

As though in response to the emotional demands of the poetry, Chausson's settings in Op. 8 become more involved and complex, although these words are not used in a derogatory sense. The first of the four, *Nocturne* (1886), has interesting cross-rhythms throughout that occur as a result of the interaction between the flowing eighth-note acccmpaniment and the vocal line. The former begins innocently enough two measures before the entry of the voice with a figure consisting of high chords and two lower single notes; the effect is of triplets in $\frac{3}{4}$ meter. However, the meter is not $\frac{3}{4}$ but $\frac{4}{4}$, so that when the voice enters, the cross-rhythms commence because of the very usual and regular quadruple patterns to which the poem is set. Later in the song there are interior cross-rhythms in the accompaniment itself that interact still more interestingly with the vocal line. Chausson's direction, *très égal et sans nuances,* shows that he was aware of the problems; his wishes are carried out dynamically as well, for except for a brief *forte* near the end, the song is very quiet. The overall effect of the rhythmic undercurrents and the dynamic markings is to underline the restlessness in the poem, which is about the moody night and a dying love.

Amour d'antan, second in the set, seems to be a mixture of styles—principally the cloying sweetness of Massenet plus the briefest touch of Debussy's dominant ninths. There is too much filler material from time to time in the accompaniment, and some of the chromatic modulations seem rather forced. On the positive side, Chausson has obviously tried to capture the vague, unsubstantial dream world of the poem in a delicate, at times almost fragile, texture.

With *Printemps triste* (1883–88) we are suddenly in another world—that of Wagner's *Tristan und Isolde.* It is not at all surprising that this world should appear sooner or later in Chausson's music; one need only refer to the excerpts from his letters to realize how unrelenting the battle was. That Chausson was far from alone in this struggle is made abundantly clear in documentary form by Elliott Zuckerman in his valuable work, *The First Hundred Years of Wagner's*

Fig. 3. Chausson; *Nocturne,* mm. 19–23

Tristan; among others, d'Indy, Chabrier, and Debussy were affected. It is appropriate at this point to examine the Wagnerian influence on Chausson in some detail.

In his study of the powerful effects of *Tristan* on persons in all walks of artistic life, Zuckerman distinguishes between what he terms "Wagnerism" and "Tristanism." The former is concerned with the aesthetic, political, and philosophical ideas of Wagner, and would be "a history of doctrines and movements: Symbolism, Naturalism, Aestheticism; anti-Semitism, Nazism, the Cult of Bayreuth. Within that history

Tristan would have to be set apart." Concerning "Tristan-ism," Zuckerman asserts that it

> begins with a direct response to the music. It is private rather than public, the result of a personal infatuation rather than an ideological commitment. Its history is not social but biographical. The Wagnerite must learn theories and cultivate habits. The Tristanite only has to be over-whelmed. . . . A composer could find the music of *Tristan* obtrusively recurring in his own. This happened to Emman-uel Chabrier and Ernest Chausson, later to Arnold Schoen-berg, and in some degree to almost every composer who worked between 1880 and 1910.[12]

That the effect of *Tristan* on composers is essentially harmonic is a fact that needs no defense. While it is no doubt true that it was the combination and interaction of melodic, rhythmic, and harmonic elements—the work as a whole—that overwhelmed Tristanites like Chabrier and Lekeu, it is equally true that it is the harmony of *Tristan* that has appeared in other composers' works and engaged the atten-tion of writers and commentators because it is too distinctive to be ignored. Its power is implied when Zuckerman ob-serves that "words can convey little meaning when they are prolonged as they are in Brangaene's warning song, or dis-torted as they are at the climax of the love-duet, where they are further disguised by canonic imitation," and adds "but in both cases the orchestra is sounding its richest harmon-ies."[13]

Grout is more explicit about the *Tristan* harmony when he writes:

> The dominant mood is conveyed in a chromatic style of writing which is no longer either a mere decorative adjunct to, or a deliberate contrast with, a fundamentally diatonic idiom, but which is actually the norm, so much so that the few diatonic motifs are felt as deliberate departures, "specters of day" intruding into the all-prevailing night of the love drama. . . . The power of the *Tristan* chroma-

ticism comes from its being founded in tonality. A feature
of it is the ambiguity of the chords, the constant, imma-
nent, felt possibility that almost any chord may resolve in
almost any one of a dozen different directions. Yet this
very ambiguity could not exist except for underlying tonal
relations, the general tendencies of certain chord progressions within the tonal system.[14]

The most obvious harmonic reference to Wagner and
the one most frequently encountered in Chausson's music
is the chord in the second measure of the *Tristan* Prelude.
This chord, shown below and hereinafter referred to as the
Tristan Chord, consists of two fourths—one augmented,

the other perfect. It has been, and still is, a subject of contro-
versy among theorists as to its classification and resolution.
For purposes of comparison, Gerald Abraham presents
shortened versions of three analyses of the chord—those
of Donald Tovey, George Dyson, and Ernst Kurth;[15] each
of these interpretations is widely different from the others.
A recent work that once again deals with the problem is Martin Vogel's *Der Tristan-Akkord und die Krise der modernen
Harmonie-Lehre.*[16] The whole question of how to classify
the *Tristan* Chord is further complicated by the fact that when
the chord appears in different harmonic contexts and with

different spellings, it is subject to still more interpretations. It is not my purpose here to favor one analysis over another or to suggest one of my own, but rather to point out that the chord's appearance in the works of composers since Wagner and its treatment by theorists are both indicative of its importance. Even more important, the sound of the chord is so typically Wagnerian as to attract attention whenever it is heard in the music of any composer, either before or after Wagner.[17] That Wagner had shown a strong preference for the chord prior to its appearance in *Tristan* is evidenced by its use in both versions of the Venusberg music from *Tannhäuser,* and in those portions of the Ring cycle that had been completed before *Tristan.* However, its prominence in *Tristan* is assured by its position as the very first chord of the entire work. Zuckerman observes that "no tune or leitmotif could evoke the work's predominant mood so economically and no rhythmic trope could do it at all."[18] In a footnote to this passage he adds, "indeed, the chord recurs, in one inversion or another, at almost every important place in the score."[19] Thus, given the overwhelming emotional climate of *Tristan,* the use of this distinctive chord by other composers (when they found themselves writing in a similarly emotional vein) seemed natural and proved almost impossible to resist.

The *Tristan* Chord appears to have been highly favored by Chausson, to judge from the fact that it appears in the majority of his *mélodies*—twenty-seven of the published songs. The number of times it is found in each *mélodie* ranges from one in *Le Charme* to fifteen in *Printemps triste.* These appearances are all the more surprising in view of Chausson's awareness of Wagner's power to influence his music; apparently he failed to see that the sound of the *Tristan* Chord is one of the most recognizable characteristics of Wagner's style. However, in fairness to Chausson, it must be noted that not all appearances of the chord are equally conspicuous, for the harmonic context of which the chord is a part helps to determine the degree of prominence. These contexts are frequently different—some being diatonic as in *Le Charme,* while those in *Printemps triste* are chromatic. In the former context the chord stands out sometimes startlingly, while in the latter it blends in with its surroundings, although it is never submerged to the point where there is difficulty in recognizing it.

In *Printemps triste,* one of the most Wagnerian of all Chausson's *mélodies,* the *Tristan* Chord appears fifteen times in the song's forty-two measures. While this is in itself enough to impart a distinctive flavor, other Wagnerian factors are also at work in conjunction with the chord. In Figure 4, where the first sequence from the song is shown, the chord appears on the third beats of measures 5, 7, and 9. The additional elements that contribute to the Wagnerian atmosphere are the harmonic uncertainties—represented by the consecutive diminished sevenths—in the transitions between C minor and F minor, and between the latter and B-flat minor; and the appoggiatura treatment and resolution of the final diminished seventh in measures 6 and 8. And, of course, the restless modulations of this passage to which the diminished sevenths contribute and of which the appoggiaturas and *Tristan* Chords are a part are themselves a Wagnerian trait.

Another passage near the end of *Printemps triste* (measures 33-34) is also strongly Wagnerian in character, although no direct references to a specific passage in Wagner come to mind. However, the emotional intensity of the excerpt—particularly in the falling arpeggios of the *Tristan* Chord—inevitably suggests the climax of the *Tristan* Prelude (measures 81-83).

Above this rather thick-textured accompaniment the vocal line moves in a parlando style that contains many repeated notes. Its chromaticism follows that of the accompaniment and emphasizes still more the gloomy nostalgia of Bouchor's poem. The latter is simply too romantic to be expressed in anything but the most general terms, and Chaus-

Fig. 4. Chausson; *Printemps triste,* mm. 5–9

son seems to have realized this by giving the poem a setting whose almost impenetrable texture matches perfectly the impenetrable atmosphere Bouchor created.

In view of the above, it is interesting and revealing to learn of Bouchor's anti-Wagner sentiments, expressed in 1884; whether they were directed at Chausson's setting of *Printemps triste* is not known. They could have been, because, although the completion date for Chausson's *mélodie* was 1888, the composer had begun to set the poem in 1883. At any rate, Bouchor spoke of his great dislike of Wagner and denounced him for his "glorification of the idiot (*Parsifal*), his hatred of day (*Tristan*), his renunciation of all sorts of things (Niebelungen)." He went on to say rather pointedly to Chausson, "your chromaticism fills me with horror."[20]

Nos Souvenirs, last of the set, has an accompaniment that, except for the rather lengthy piano epilogue, is as uniformly thin as that of *Printemps triste* is dense. This thinness is emphasized from the beginning by two parallel lines of single notes that are two octaves and a third apart. Upon reading the poem, which commences with "our memories, all these things/Which we scatter into the winds/Like petals of roses,/Or wings of butterflies," one cannot but sense that Chausson is carefully attempting to delineate not only the delicacy but also the idea of distance inherent in events of a time long past. When the poem tells us that "it is astonishing/How the past reappears," there is a slight thickening and a certain solidity as the left hand firmly sits on a pedal point (G-sharp) while the right hand descends as if to emphasize returning reality. The two lines then restore the distance and the thinness, this time with the right hand playing triplets against the left hand's prevailing eighths, as though to slightly confuse things in conformity with the poem's dreamlike mood: "At certain moments it seems/That the dream lasts forever."

The piano epilogue of fourteen measures, an excerpt from which is shown in Figure 5, is an example of almost complete syncopation. Although the first and second beats of each measure are defined, they are of secondary importance when compared to the emphases of the displaced chords moving in a separate rhythmic pattern. The sudden change to sixteenth notes in the epilogue seems again to demonstrate Chausson's sensitivity to the text, for the poem

ends with "a fluttering of wings/That returns from the happy
past."

Fig. 5. Chausson; *Nos Souvenirs,* mm. 74–76

Four *mélodies* comprise Op. 13, the first of which—*Apaisement* (1885)—is also Chausson's first setting of a Verlaine
poem; there were destined to be but two more. Just why the
composer set so few poems by one of France's great poets is
a mystery, but his failure to set more has left us impover-
ished, for in all three instances his settings are superior.

The word *apaisement* occurs near the end of "La Lune
blanche," one of the poems from Verlaine's cycle, *La Bonne
Chanson,* and was chosen as a title by Chausson perhaps
because the word reflected his conception of the poem's
essential meaning. Fauré also set the poem, using its original
title, and there are two other settings to the title "L'Heure
exquise," the poem's final words; one by Reynaldo Hahn,
the other by Poldowski.[21] Chausson's setting is dedicated to
Camille Benoît, one of the Franckists.

The quality that makes *Apaisement* a superior *mélodie*
is just that element which distinguishes all outstanding
French art, whether it be literature, painting, or music:

suggestion, understatement. And Chausson's *mélodie* a-
chieves this quality because its composer took his cue from
Verlaine's power to suggest and understate, and set the poem
in like manner. Conversely, the overstatement of such *mélodies* as *Printemps triste*—however expressive it might be—is
as much the fault of the poet's sentimental effusiveness as
it is Chausson's failure to recognize the "un-French" qualities of the poem and to perceive that the resulting song is not
typically French in the best sense.

As for *Apaisement,* Chausson's writing is illustrative of
the gentle mood of the poem from the slightly restless feeling of the early lines to the utter calm of the close; gently
rocking chords containing sevenths of various kinds, and
in the middle of the song some discreet chromaticisms. All
of these elements moving in a slow harmonic rhythm with
sustained pedal points beneath, are the vehicles by which
the mood is transmitted. Also evident is Chausson's careful
attention to such details as lengths of poetic lines, where
commas are matched with short rests, while the next three
poetic lines, containing no punctuation, are set as one long
phrase.

Sérénade (1887), the second *mélodie* of Op. 13, is set to a
poem by the Parnassian poet Jean Lahor, the pen-name
of Henri Cazalis, who was a friend of Mallarmé, a society
doctor, and a medical consultant at Aix-les-Bains, where
he attended Verlaine. The song is dedicated to Maurice
Bagès de Trigny, the singer and frequenter of 22 Boulevard
de Courcelles, mentioned earlier as having been an outstanding interpreter of *mélodies.*

Sérénade is a combination of two seemingly irreconcilable elements: an accompaniment with abrupt, unprepared
modulations and several instances of the *Tristan* Chord,
together with an unmistakable modality in both the accompaniment and the vocal line. Of these two elements, it is the
modality that is the more unusual, for it imparts a special
flavor to the song, which is nominally in E major. However,

in both of the relatively stable E-major portions (measures 1–13, 45 to the end at 58), D, C, and F- natural are consistently employed in both vocal line and accompaniment; G-natural is also found occasionally. A corresponding lowering of accidentals occurs when F major and D major are established as temporary tonics. Thus a rather uniform Phrygian sound is achieved; indeed, shortly after the beginning the voice outlines a complete, downward-moving Phrygian scale. Also worthy of mention is the constant eighth-note motion, which never abates and which produces a soothing, flowing, and gently undulating character. Another distinctive sound that contributes greatly to the expressive qualities of the song is the consistent use of appoggiaturas on the first half of many of the second beats in the right-hand part. Taken as a whole, the disparate elements of *Sérénade* combine harmoniously in such a manner as to produce a unity that becomes more satisfying with each hearing.

L'Aveu (1887), dedicated to Chausson's close friend Paul Poujaud, was set to a poem by the Breton nobleman and Symbolist Villiers de l'Isle-Adam (1838–89) who, in addition to his activities as a poet, was a novelist and dramatist. It is in the last capacity that he is chiefly remembered, for his poetic drama *Axel* (1890) exerted a strong influence on the Symbolist movement; its message of resignation is found on a much smaller scale in *L'Aveu*.

From a formal standpoint, the song's structure is different from any encountered in Chausson's *mélodies,* most of which are modified ternary or through-composed. Here, the plan is ABAB, where both A sections are in $\frac{3}{4}$ meter while each B section is in $\frac{6}{8}$ meter. The first A is slightly longer (seventeen measures) than the second (fourteen measures); both are marked *très lent*. Each B section is marked *plus vite,* but with thirty-nine measures the second B is more than twice as long as the first B (fifteen measures). There are wide discrepancies between the musical material of each A and each B, because each of these sections is identical for only the first four or five measures. Thus the structure is really somewhat looser than it appears to be.

The hearer is immediately aware of a heavy, chromatic texture, not so consistent and uniform as that of *Printemps triste* but with similar references to Wagner and, this time, to Franck. Let us consider the Franckian resemblances first. The melody of the accompaniment in the first five measures bears a family relationship to the theme of Franck's Symphony in D minor, second movement, by virtue of the tendency, so often seen in Franck, to centralize a theme around one note by returning to that note on accented beats (A in *L'Aveu,* F in the Symphony). In addition, some of the chromatic harmonies are similar to Franck's, for if we compare the little bracketed figures in the following example, it will be seen that they proceed from and return to the same harmonic context. Franck has sounded his momentary tonic—C-sharp major—on the last beat of the measure preceding the example and, as we see, returns to it a measure later. If we change this tonic to minor in agreement with Chausson's, the harmony between statements of the tonic is the same in both passages: submediant with a lowered third. In addition, the root position of this chord and the presence of the same intervals and direction in the top lines emphasize the similarity.

Fig. 6. Chausson; *L'Aveu,* mm. 3–5
   Franck; Quintet, 1, m. 92

Another chromatic passage with strong resemblances to Franck may be seen in measures 41-44, where the similarities are to the latter's *Prelude, Chorale, and Fugue* for piano (1884). This work contains harmonic chromaticism that assumes a larger and more important role than it did in some of Franck's previous pieces because it pervades wider areas of the composition. This is particularly true of the fugue, whose melodically chromatic subject invites and receives almost continuous chromatic treatment in its harmonic structure. The passage from *L'Aveu* occurs halfway through the song and appears below in Figure 7 together with a passage from the first section of Franck's work. Although the two passages are not at all related thematically, there is a family resemblance in that each contains a melodic top line that is chromatic (Franck's more than Chausson's); a winding, chromatic middle line in which the emphasis is contrapuntal; and diminished harmony approached and quitted by means of chromatic voice-leading (marked in the examples). As far as Chausson is concerned, this is the first *mélodie* in which such a tightly knit chromatic passage is to be found.

The Wagnerian passages are also two in number, the first occurring in measures 7-9, where the reference to the *Tristan* Prelude is startling. The second passage, although less directly quoted, is similar to the third act transformation scene in *Parsifal*—the gradual change from the temple grounds to the interior of the Grail Temple itself. Both passages begin with the *Tristan* Chord. The reference to *Parsifal* rather than *Tristan* is not strange when it is understood that there is an enthusiasm for *Parsifal* among French musicians that, according to Oscar Thompson, shows itself "in a manner and to a degree so rapturous as to bewilder their fellow Wagnerians in other lands."[22]

The final *mélodie* of Op. 13, *La Cigale* (*The Grasshopper*), is all happiness and sunlight. The poem by the Parnassian Leconte de Lisle is classically restrained and contains appropriate references to the ancient world. Chausson matches

Fig. 7. Chausson; *L'Aveu,* mm. 41–44
    Franck; *Prelude, Chorale, and Fugue,* mm. 31–32

this mood with a $\frac{6}{8}$ setting marked *gaiment,* in which the opening piano melody, reproduced exactly in the voice a few measures later, is partly Mixolydian. Surprisingly, an arpeggiated *Tristan* Chord appears (measures 54–55) in the midst of a diatonic fabric. However, in sum, *La Cigale* is one of Chausson's most spontaneous *mélodies.*

La Caravane (1887), although no longer than some of Chausson's other *mélodies,* is assigned an opus number (14) by itself. Whether this isolation was intended to suggest that the composer considered this song to be more important than some of the others is not known. A possible answer in support of such a theory is provided by the poem to which *La Caravane* is set. By Gautier, it describes the heavy plodding of "the human caravan in the Sahara of the world." There is no shade but that of the vulture, while at the end of the journey there is "a cypress wood sown with white tombstones" provided by the Lord as a means of attaining rest "in the desert of time." It is a bleak picture whose pessimistic philosophy of unremitting struggle may have found an answering vibration in Chausson's experience, thus dictating an isolated position in his oeuvre.

Another possible answer to the question is provided by the dedication to Ernest van Dyke, a Belgian tenor who attained some importance and fame as a Wagnerian interpreter. According to one account van Dyck

> first studied law, then took up journalism in Antwerp and Paris. He was taught singing by Saint-Yves Bax in Paris, and in 1883 made his debut at the Concerts Lamoureux [in Beethoven's Ninth Symphony]. He made his stage debut in the famous production of *Lohengrin* at the Eden Theatre on May 3, 1887, and in 1888 appeared as Parsifal at Bayreuth with extraordinary success (he had studied the role under Mottl).[23]

Van Dyck's later career took him to New York's Metropolitan Opera where, from 1898 to 1902, he appeared in Wagnerian roles as well as in various French operas. An intimate friend of Chabrier, van Dyck had also been associated with Debussy in the days before the latter achieved fame. Chausson admired him greatly, and he was a guest at 22 Boulevard de Courcelles.

Again, as in *L'Aveu,* there are specific references to Wagner and Franck, the more noticeable because of the almost continuous transitions and modulations in the heavy, chordal accompaniment. In the case of the Franckian references the similarities are brought about by the same chromatic techniques as those found in Franck's sequential writing, where the harmony is treated as a unit that is often raised or lowered bodily, and where literal transpositions are the norm. Until this point in Chausson's *mélodie* writing, his sequences had all been of a diatonic and quite relaxed type, in which the transpositions of the basic sequential pattern were not only not literal repetitions but sometimes concerned one part only, the others being occupied with repeated notes on the same pitch, pedal points, and the like. In *La Caravane,* however, Chausson's sequential writing has become like Franck's even to the point of employing the latter's customarily short sequential pattern—one measure. All this brings to mind again Franck's *Prelude, Chorale, and Fugue,* for here in Chausson's *mélodie* the general style of piano writing is the same as that of the Franck work: large chords, wide spacing, general massiveness, and deep sonorities.

Strikingly parallel passages involving *La Caravane* and the Franck work just mentioned represent perhaps the high-water mark in terms of Chausson passages that sound and even look Franckian: the first of these is shown in Figure 8. Here the chromatic descents, the appoggiatura treatment (Chausson's top line, Franck's bass line), and the general textures are certainly alike. Still another startlingly similar parallelism occurs in measures 36–37, where a portion of Franck's fugue subject appears in Chausson's song; not only is the metrical position identical, but the harmony at the beginning of the second measure is almost note for note the same. However, even though *La Caravane* contains more Franckian reminiscences than any other Chausson *mélodie,* they are isolated instances, for in their position in the music's flow they neither proceed from nor progress to that special fusion of harmonic factors that is peculiar to Franck and that makes his style instantly recognizable.

The Wagnerian references in *La Caravane* are not to *Tristan* but to the two instrumental sections in *Parsifal*—one in the first, the other in the third act—that serve as transitions while Gurnemanz and Parsifal slowly walk from the

Fig. 8. Chausson; *La Caravane,* mm. 45–47
　　　Franck; *Prelude, Chorale, and Fugue,* mm. 358–59

grounds of the Grail Temple to that point inside the temple
where the suffering of the stricken Amfortas will be revealed
to all of the assembled knights. As the two men slowly move
toward their objective, Wagner's music subtly changes from
a diatonic to a chromatic texture. The same sort of chromaticism finds its way into *La Caravane* in what is perhaps
not an accidental manner, for the text of Chausson's *mélodie,* like the chromatic passages in these sections of *Parsifal,*
is concerned with suffering—specifically, that of the human
race as it plods in a caravan across the desert of this world.

The first noticeable resemblance to *Parsifal* occurs in the first few measures of *La Caravane,* the reference being to the second of Wagner's transformation scenes. In Figure 9, where a passage from each work is shown, it will be noted that Chausson, like Wagner, employs a triplet figure on the fourth beat of the measure. In the examples the harmony of each composer's first two measures is very similar and, of course, the chord at the beginning of the third measures is identical. Other passages in *La Caravane* are less literal, but because of the frequent use of the triplet figure and the type of chromaticism seen in Figure 9 there is an almost continuous Wagnerian sound for fully two thirds of the song.

Fig. 9. Chausson; *La Caravane,* mm. 2–4
Wagner; *Parsifal,* 3, p. 255, mm. 19–21

The year 1888 saw the completion of Op. 17, the two *Chansons de Miarka*—"Les Morts" and "La Pluie"—to poems of Jean Richepin. After the complexities of *La Caravane* both are delightfully simple. The message of "Les Morts" is that the dead will live, poetically expressed by a kiss passed from mouth to mouth. Chausson's setting features a placid four-measure figure that unifies the *mélodie* by appearing in both voice and accompaniment at intervals all the way through the song, now in one key, now in another. The harmonies are simple throughout and include nothing more complicated than a few seventh chords and one or two very brief passages of melodic chromaticism.

"La Pluie," to a poem describing rain falling on dead leaves, dust, and grain, has an accompaniment whose consistent sixteenth-note movement strongly suggests pentatonicism. This extremely rare quality in Chausson's music is made more prominent in "La Pluie" by being sounded in octaves and occasionally echoed in the vocal line. It is nowhere so explicit and pervasive as it is in certain Debussy works, but its delicate suggestiveness here helps to strengthen the thesis proposed by G. Jean-Aubry and Arthur Hoerée that Chausson was a connecting link between Franck and Debussy.[24] This is in direct contradiction to Norman Demuth's statement that "between the Impressionists and the Franckists there is a great gulf fixed with nothing in common to bridge it except a love of music."[25]

It may very well be that Chausson was not consciously creating a pentatonic atmosphere in "La Pluie," although in the very next year—1889—he did include an all "black note" pentatonic melody (with the single exception of the final note) in the first movement of his Symphony in B-flat major, a circumstance that does not appear to be accidental. French musicians by this time were becoming well aware of Oriental music for, according to Vallas, "during the summer of 1887, Julien Tiersot devoted important articles to it in the *Ménestrel.*"[26] And, of course, there was the Exposition Universelle of 1889 that fascinated Debussy with its Gamelang orchestra and groups of Oriental performers, and to which he returned again and again. In contrast to Debussy's curiosity and fascination, it is a little disappointing to find that the only reference to a Chausson visit indicates that it was short and that it was made in the company of his wife and largely for her pleasure.[27] This seems strange in view of Chausson's intellectual curiosity, so aptly demonstrated by his large library; yet there is a vast difference between reading about something and experiencing it personally. It is very possible that Chausson visited the Exposition more than just this one time without leaving any record of such visits.

It is interesting to speculate that Debussy may have profited from certain corners of Chausson's library to a greater degree than its owner for, in an exhaustive article containing almost two hundred musical examples and entitled "Pentatony in Debussy's Music," Constantin Brailoïu makes the significant statement that "we may possibly also remember Debussy's erudite friend Chausson, proprietor of a library of folklore, whose books might have passed through the composer's hands."[28] Although the dispersal of Chausson's library probably prevents our ever learning the titles and nature of these books, the very fact of their presence indicates their owner's interest in the subject.

Poème de l'amour et de la mer, Op. 19, is one of Chausson's longest and most ambitious works. Begun in the summer of 1882, it occupied him at intervals until June 1890; it was revised in June 1893. Conceived for voice and orchestra, it is a setting of two long poems by Bouchor—"La Fleur des eaux" and "La Mort de l'amour"—separated by an orchestral interlude. The final third of the second *mélodie,* beginning with the words "Le Temps des lilas," has been published separately under that title with piano accompaniment. The work was first performed in Brussels on February 21, 1893, in a piano version played by Chausson but with the interlude omitted because he felt too unsure of himself; the singer was Désiré Demest, a tenor. The first performance with orchestra took place at the Société Nationale in April 1893; in the summer of that year the Concerts Ysaÿe played it in Brussels.

The work was dedicated to Henri Duparc who, however, had certain reservations with respect to the fitting of the music to the text:

> In short—and this is perhaps clearer—I had more than once the impression that the words had been *adapted* to the music and that there was not absolute cohesion between the two; I know well, that goes without saying, that you do not write the music first and attach the words to it later; but perhaps you hasten too much to think of the music before having sufficiently penetrated the words and declaimed them to yourself as they are.
> . . . Believe me, do not write the music of one line without declaiming it to yourself aloud, with the accents and the gestures. Reread the *Poème* from this point of view and I think that, now I have called your attention to it, you will understand better by yourself what I mean than with the aid of my hieroglyphics.[29]

Duparc's criticism is well-founded for, here and there, the music does violate the natural accents of the words, the obvious reason being that not every appearance of the two themes Chausson employs as the unifying agents in such a long work is always suited to the text at a particular point. Instances where words and music do not match occur at important places in "Le Temps des lilas," the concluding section, where the second theme assumes its final and definitive form; each time the theme is set to words the natural accentuation is upset (Figure 10). However, the theme is so beautiful in itself and so strikingly suited to the haunted text that such slight lapses seem unimportant. Indeed, the music of the *Poéme* as a whole is so far superior to Bouchor's melodramatic poems about "the inexpressible horrors of dead loves" that one is somehow carried along by its expansive sweep and tends to ignore the poetry to which it is set. And yet the poetry compels our attention and respect because Chausson's music gives it life it otherwise would not have, a life breathed into it at almost every point by a composer who was sensitively responsive to it.

Fig. 10. Chausson; *Le Temps des lilas,* mm. 5–8

Just how perceptive Chausson was with respect to Bouchor's poems is demonstrated by the care taken to match music and poetry at all the external structural points. Each one of the two poems has three broad but unequal divisions: thirteen, eight, and twenty lines for the first; nine, fourteen, and sixteen lines for the second. In each poem the emotional climate changes from the general to the particular; from the sunlit boisterousness of the sea in the first poem and the calm, amethyst sea in the second to the deep personal grief at the end of both as love ebbs away from vibrant life to empty hopelessness. Chausson's music mirrors these changes faithfully and dramatically, principally by means of the orchestra.

In fact, the orchestra looms large in Chausson's thinking, for it is no mere pallid accompaniment to the vocal line but a large force in which all the instrumental colors and resources are used with boldness, yet discretion. Between the main textual divisions noted above Chausson has provided rather lengthy orchestral passages that begin in the mood of the text just concluded and progress to the mood of the text about to be sung, a procedure that immediately calls to mind the similar technique in Debussy's *Pelléas et Mélisande* some years later.

The origin in the orchestra of much of the principal generating material is, of course, an important Wagnerian technique, one of which Chausson must have been well aware. However, there are no *leitmotifs;* in their place are two expansive main themes that sound in varied form in strategic places (the second of these appeared in Figure 10). The first one is associated with the sea and adapts itself to its moods, while the second is elegiac; the vocal line shares both themes with the orchestra. Much of the remainder of the orchestral fabric is taken up with an "endless melody" type of texture—another Wagnerian trait. And here and there the language is Wagnerian, recalling *Tristan* and *Parsifal,* the latter especially in the section immediately preceding "Le Temps des lilas," where the anguish of dead loves is expressed in heavy, lifeless terms after an emotional climax that has overtones of the Amfortas music. And yet, much of the music is not Wagnerian at all but French in its delicacy, with even a certain objectivity. The vocal line is often rather high, where it stands out in great clarity against the orchestra. It is finely wrought and has a French elegance to it with its long, spun-out phrases.

It seems a shame that such a well-composed work, one that really "sounds" in performance and that maintains a momentum to the end is largely unknown except for the *mélodie* that forms its last section and that was extracted from it. Thus we should be very grateful to Victoria de los Angeles and the

Lamoureux Orchestra for their excellent recorded performance of the entire work; let us hope that the recording will stimulate a new interest in *Poème de l'amour et de la mer,* with live performances as the outcome.

After the *Chansons de Miarka* of 1888, there is a five-year period during which Chausson was occupied with various other projects—the Symphony, Concert in D major, *La Légende de Sainte Cécile,* and so on—and, therefore wrote no *mélodies* for voice and piano. When he did return to the genre in 1893, it was to set five of Maurice Maeterlinck's enigmatic *Serres chaudes (Hot-Houses).*

Concerning these poems, W. D. Halls writes that they "betrayed a mind at the end of its tether and, in the wildness of its imaginings, near to dementia."[30] Barricelli and Weinstein speak of Maeterlinck's "dream-ridden poems" and of Chausson's settings that "had to express the haunts of mystery and the vague fears before the unknown that characterize the text: moments of weariness and ennui, of sadness, of fever, of prayer."[31] The composer had been introduced to *Serres chaudes* by his good friend and staunch admirer Octave Maus, the Belgian art critic and founder of the Libre Esthétique of Brussels, where a number of Chausson works, including *Poème de l'amour et de la mer,* were first performed.

That Chausson had serious misgivings about his settings of these poems is indicated by the following lines written to Debussy: "I shall send them to you not without uneasiness. Only one thing delights me about them—it is that I do not have to fear hearing them sung in concert"; he considered them to be "too difficult for performance and also too hermetic to be intelligible to the public."[32] However, they were given a first hearing at the Société Nationale on April 3, 1897, by Thérèse Roger (to whom the cycle is dedicated) and the pianist Edouard Risler; it can be assumed that Chausson was present despite his reservations. Whether or not Debussy was is not known, for the two composers had separated in 1894 because of Debussy's broken engagement to Mlle Roger. But Debussy, fortunately, did not allow this unpleasantness to prejudice his generally favorable impressions of *Serres chaudes,* written in *Gil Blas* for March 30, 1903: "these *mélodies* are little dramas whose passionate metaphysics Chausson brings out without overemphasis. One could wish that he had given more liberty to all that intimate emotion which vibrates in his very individual interpretation." [33]

D'Indy felt that Chausson had never attained a more complete correspondence between words and music, and speaks enthusiastically of the affinity between the minds of the two artists. [34] If such an affinity exists, it represents a departure from Chausson's expressed desire for poetry with relatively simple imagery and uncomplicated emotions. Of course, as noted earlier, Oulmont remarked that he was the first to understand Maeterlinck, and the same author is also authority for the statement that Chausson discovered in these poems "above all an excuse to satisfy his inclinations towards mysticism." [35] But Oulmont also feels that "without doubt, Chausson was under no illusions with respect to the deep worth of the poetic text;" then he adds the composer's words to Gustave Samazeuilh, "but the work lends itself to musical treatment." [36] Perhaps the challenge implicit in this last statement is the ultimate answer to the elusive question as to what Chausson found in these poems. From the vantage ground of almost a century later, Maeterlinck's texts appear to be as obscure as those of Mallarmé, a poet Chausson never set and to whom he was obviously referring when he wrote to Raymond Bonheur, "Do you not know a modern poet who puts too many topazes in his verse?" [37] In a letter to the present author Jean Gallois explains that Mallarmé's art was too dry, too abstract for Chausson, who was far more responsive to the heart than to things intellectual; he did not know how to thread his way through abstract verse, and Mallarmé's poetry did not touch him emotionally. On the other hand, Maeterlinck's imagery is more concrete and thus emotional, even though it is highly symbolic in a privately conceived mystical world. Even so, Chausson wisely refrained from any attempt to portray the text too literally; he sought instead to transfer to his settings the general Symbolist atmosphere of ennui, melancholy, and unexplained dread. As Gallois puts it, "in the face of Maeterlinck's universe, voluntarily mysterious, filled with vague fears and concealing long periods of fever, of melancholy, or of simple spleen, not much 'plastic description' is possible. The evocation of emotions poorly defined resides solely on the musical plane where there stirs an undefined sensitivity little concerned with tangible reality."[38]

Undoubtedly because of the vagueness of the subject matter, certain passages of *Serres chaudes* attain a complexity not hitherto seen in Chausson's *mélodies,* but to lump all five settings together and label their textures as "unbearably thick and heavy"[39] seems excessive and unfair. The longest and most complex of all is "Serre chaude," the first *mélodie* of the cycle but the last to be completed (1896). The first to be finished were "Lassitude" (June 30, 1893) and "Serre d'ennui" (July 7, 1893), third and second of the set; "Fauves las" and "Oraison," fourth and fifth of the set, were finished February 27, 1896.

The dates for "Lassitude" and "Serre d'ennui" and the place where they were composed—Luzancy—may be significant. Luzancy was the large country estate on the Marne that Chausson's in-laws had rented for the summers of 1892 and 1893. Its proximity to Paris made it readily accessible to visitors, and the late spring of 1893 saw Debussy there as a house guest. At Chausson's request he had brought along a copy of Moussorgsky's *Boris Godunov,* the same copy of the original edition that Saint-Saëns had brought back from Moscow in 1874. Saint-Saëns, "who was too conservative to appreciate such a very daring work, had given this copy—then unique in France—to Jules de Brayer, an

organist [at Chartres] and professor of music, who was man-
ager of the Concerts Lamoureux, and a contributor to the
Revue Wagnérienne."[40] De Brayer soon became one of
Moussorgsky's most ardent supporters. According to Lockspeiser, "the first performance of a work of Moussorgsky
in France consisted of a fragment of *Boris* played on the
organ of the Trocadéro in Paris by Jules de Brayer on 7
November, 1878."[41] In due time the score of *Boris* came
into the possession of Debussy's close friend Robert Godet,
the Swiss author of a two-volume work called *En Marge de
"Boris Godounow,"* who, in turn, loaned or gave it to Debussy around 1890. It was not until 1893 at Luzancy that
Debussy read the score through completely in the presence
of Chausson. One can assume that *Boris* is the work being
played at the piano in the famous photograph where Chausson turns pages for Debussy while the Henri Lerolles, Raymond Bonheur, and Mme Chausson look on, although one
cannot be certain. In an undated letter written in 1893 before Debussy's visit, Chausson says, "and perhaps the new
Moussorgsky scores will be here. Borrow all the Russian
music you can find."[42] What Chausson's exposure to Russian music had been prior to Debussy's visit is not presently
known. Gallois's remarks seem to indicate an earlier knowledge of *Boris* in Paris, where Debussy had shown Chausson
the score.[43] At any rate, the fruits of this Russian encounter
via Debussy appear in "Lassitude," which has an unmistakable Russian flavor.

The ingredients that combine to produce this flavor are a
terse, four-note, scalewise, ascending motive frequently
followed by an abrupt falling figure; a rather consistent use
of pedal points throughout much of the song; a tendency
to return to the tonic note except in brief passages where
new keys are sounded abruptly, no modulation having
taken place; and an alternation of $\frac{3}{2}$ and $\frac{2}{2}$ meters that
in places has the effect of an overall $\frac{5}{2}$ scheme. When the

lowered second degree (the key is F-sharp minor) is present in both accompaniment and vocal line directly after the four-note motive (the latter is confined to the piano part), the modal effect is unmistakable. Although no particular Moussorgsky passages come to mind as possible models for Chausson, each of the techniques noted above—modality, motivic writing, pedal points, sudden key-assumptions, and alternations of meters—occurs in *Boris Godunov* and other works such as *Songs and Dances of Death.* When they are all present together, as they are in portions of "Lassitude," the effect is noticeably Russian.

From an expressive viewpoint, Chausson's *mélodie* has a distinctive Russian flavor, created by the combination of the heavy pedal points when they are sounded in both hands, and the limited range of the voice part. The lifelessness of the poem is conveyed in a vocal line consisting of a rather large number of repeated notes in a generally undulating pattern in which any skip larger than a major third is exceptional; all these melodic characteristics are also Moussorgskyian. Together with Chausson's directions—*calme,* and *très lié* (very legato)—the emotional content is one of heaviness, gloom, and a certain fatalism. Although we have met these qualities in some of Chausson's earlier *mélodies*— *Printemps triste, Caravane,* and *Poème de l'amour et de la mer*—they have been expressed in more conventional musical terms, indeed, in what one can legitimately call "western European" terms. "Lassitude" stands out from these other *mélodies* by virtue of a fundamentally different approach resulting in a different sound that could not have appeared out of nowhere, its Moussorgskyian properties miraculously materializing out of thin air. It is, rather, the product of an encounter with the mind of a genius, a mind Chausson was quick to recognize for its originality as it went about the business of assembling conventional musical elements in a new synthesis. Because of Chausson's fascination with this new language, "Lassitude" is one of his most interesting and effective *mélodies,* and curiously right even for its French text. It was an experiment that was not repeated.

Fig. 11. Chausson; *Lassitude,* mm. 1–3

Debussy's presence at Luzancy in the early summer of 1893 is also apparent in "Serre d'ennui," second *mélodie* of *Serres chaudes.* Here there is a sudden proliferation of major dominant ninth chords—ten altogether—whereas in all of the preceding *mélodies* they are few and far between. How else to account for them except through Debussy's visit, during which, we can be sure, the entire household was treated to his famous improvisations full of dominant ninths, whole-tone and modal passages, parallel progressions and all the other Debussy paraphernalia? Such an explanation may not be so naive and simplistic as it seems, for it hinges on documented evidence that Chausson was well aware of the dangers involved in maintaining too close a contact with Debussy's evolving style. This evidence, like that which documents Chausson's fear of Wagner, is in the form of a letter. Written to Henri Lerolle on November 28, 1893, just a few months after the Luzancy summer, there are these blunt words concerning Debussy: "he is grieved that I refuse to hear his *Pelléas et Mélisande.* Certainly this hearing has made me fearful. I am sure in advance that his music will please me very much and I am afraid of being upset with respect to my poor *Arthus,* so tossed about after a year."[44]

The performance referred to by Chausson was a private one, probably held at the Paris home of their mutual friend, Pierre Louÿs, with Debussy singing the parts and accompanying himself on either Louÿs's piano or his harmonium. Henri de Régnier tells how at Pierre Louÿs's he "often saw him at the piano. I heard him play his Baudelaire songs, extracts from 'Tristan', and most of 'Pelléas', while it was in process of composition. . . ."[45] The painter Jacques-Émile Blanche also describes these scenes when Debussy accompanied himself on Louÿs's harmonium— "a wretched instrument which the writer kept till his death," according to Vallas—and where he would " 'murmur, in his curious, timbreless voice, the freshly written scenes from *Pelléas.* The Sunday-school harmonium was transformed into a supernatural instrument.' A few painters and poets, and a very few musicians, were thus vouchsafed a revelation of the new art for which the general public had to wait ten years."[46] There is no record of Chausson's attending any of these sessions; but even if he had been able to overcome his fears of being swayed by Debussy's music, the coming breach between the two composers would have precluded his presence.

"Serre d'ennui," like "Lassitude," is another expression of the general *fin de siècle* listlessness and passivity that characterize so much Symbolist poetry. This particular setting of that atmosphere is gentler, lighter, and less insistent than that of "Lassitude." Here the texture is often arpeggiated, while the dominant ninths impart a delicacy and lightness missing from the other *mélodie;* the wider spacing of the entire accompaniment also contributes to the lightness. The unsettled, uneasy atmosphere of the poem is conveyed by a very chromatic vocal line and, in the accompaniment, by a gently rocking eighth-note figure in the right-hand part; each appearance of the figure is separated by an eighth rest.

Of the remaining three songs in the cycle, the first, "Serre chaude," was finished last (March 19, 1896), is the longest by far (seventy-nine measures), the most complex, and is the least satisfying of the set. Except for one measure near the beginning and the last ten measures, the sixteenth-note activity is continuous—an obvious attempt to match the hysteria of the poem with a steadily mounting emotional excitement in the accompaniment. The mood is broken at the end by a calm chordal section—repeated in "Oraison," the final *mélodie*—that reflects a return to sanity. The chords formed by the sixteenth-note movement and the longer values of the topmost line are various types of sevenths, augmented triads, *Tristan* Chords, as well as ordinary triads.

"Fauves las," completed February 27, 1896, has a steady triplet movement divided between the hands that contributes to the prevailing restlessness as much as do the almost continuous modulations. Only in "Oraison," begun in Florence during February 1895 and finished in Paris the same day and year as "Fauves las," is there any peace or stability. Its appeal to God is expressed in an entirely chordal texture— six-note chords are frequent—that includes a moving inner part.

Throughout all five of the *Serres chaudes* the vocal line is rhythmically very flexible, with many passages consisting of repeated sixteenths or eighths in parlando style—the type seen in Debussy's *mélodies*. The material allotted to the voice is often very chromatic, difficult enough in itself but rendered more so by the fact that the accompaniment frequently pursues its own path and thus provides no help for the singer; such obstacles undoubtedly discourage performances of the cycle. And the unevenness of the individual *mélodies* is another factor that militates against performance.

Chausson's next group of songs—oddly enough entitled *Trois Lieder*—comprise Op. 27. The poems are by the Symbolist Camille Mauclair, author—as we have seen—of the novel *Le Soleil des morts*. A close friend of Chausson's, numerous other works came from his pen: *La Religion de la musique, Les Héros de l'orchestre, La Musique française au XIXe siècle, Histoire de l'impressionnisme,* and others. He was also one of Symbolism's important theoreticians.

The first two of the *Trois Lieder*—"Les Heures" and "Ballade"—are concerned with ostinato techniques that effectively highlight their respective poems. In "Les Heures," the ostinato is both tonal and rhythmic; the syncopated and repeated A in the right hand pervades all of the twenty-and-a-half measures, while the vocal line and the left-hand part deftly weave their own material around it. The effect is somewhat similar to that of "Lassitude," but the fatigue seems less weighty and less ominous, in line with the gentle sadness of the poem. There is a more passive attitude here as the hours move, one by one, into the moonlight with sad smiles, waiting to die. Chausson's setting, aptly marked *lent et résigné,* matches this mood in its static, constantly repeating A; nowhere is the dynamic level louder than *piano.* The left hand's downward-moving chromatic line, unhurried and deliberate, adds to the pathos and melancholy of one of Chausson's finest *mélodies.*

Another highly effective *mélodie* is "Ballade," second of the set. Although it is over three times as long as "Les Heures," the rhythmic ostinato employed throughout most of it does not become tiresome because the harmonies constantly change. Because the poem centers about the sea, the gently rocking syncopated rhythms in $\frac{6}{4}$ meter enhance the scene. The poem is a novel one, refreshingly different because it is not concerned with a lost love, although loss in another sense is the subject. This time, when angels and ships become lost at sea, the birds have waited in vain for them and have then flown to the cottages and churches beside the sea to tell of the disappearance. And at night children have seen angel wings and sails of ships floating toward the stars and, in confusion and ignorance, have prayed for them. The downward-fluttering arpeggios in the final measures seem to mirror this confusion.

The final *mélodie* of Op. 27, "Les Couronnes," is Chausson's only venture into the field of popular song. The accompaniment is extremely simple with, at times, a syncopated lilt to it. Present also are seventh chords built on the tonic, supertonic, and submediant, besides other types of sevenths—all of them items in a more popular musical language. The vocal line is divided throughout into short phrases of approximately the same length, and the text is delivered in a patter of running eighth notes; these melodic features are also traits of the popular song. The entire setting is well-suited to the childlike naiveté of the poem, which tells about a little girl with three crowns—one of primrose, the second of a serrated vine, and the third fashioned from an autumn rose. The primrose was for her soul, the vine was to amuse her, and the autumn rose was for him who would be willing to love her. A handsome knight was nearby, but he did not notice her, and she let her crowns fall.

Taken as a group, the three *mélodies* of Op. 27 are among Chausson's most charming and effective; they seem to catch the innocence of the early *mélodies: Nanny, Le Charme, Les Papillons,* and others. They were first performed January 23, 1897, by Jeanne Remacle, wife of the music critic, composer, and minor literary figure Adrien Remacle. Verlaine mentions her in *Dédicaces* 27, "à Adrien Remacle," as "singing delightfully some very old verses of mine set to music by you."

When Op. 28, the four *Chansons de Shakespeare,* is examined an entirely different kind of *mélodie* presents itself. Three of the texts deal with death, while the remaining one is concerned with a lost love; the latter subject is, of course, one of Chausson's favorite themes and one he set often. However, what seems new here is the intensity of expression in all these *mélodies*. Strictly speaking, the fourth chanson, "Chant funèbre," is not a *mélodie* but a four-part women's chorus, with orchestral accompaniment by d'Indy based on Chausson's original piano part. As a member of the set it has its place here both textually and musically.

The texts are all translations by Maurice Bouchor and, with the exception of "Chanson d'Ophélie," come from the little songs that Shakespeare scattered about his dramas. The "Chanson de clown" comes from *Twelfth Night,* Act 2, Scene 4: "Come away, come away, death./ And in sad cypress let me be laid;/ Fly away, fly away, breath;/ I am slain by a fair cruel maid," and so on. It should be noted at the outset that not only this but also the three other translations are rather distressingly free renditions of the originals, and apparently strove for atmosphere rather than accuracy.

The musical setting of "Chanson de clown" represents something of a departure for Chausson, for it is essentially dramatic. As the composer's only *mélodie* written specifically for baritone, there is an admirable vocal line in declamatory style set in the medium to high range of that voice. The accompaniment is chordal, and there is a sense of spaciousness on both the horizontal and vertical planes for, with few exceptions, each measure contains but one chord, and the chords are full and sonorous. Many of the harmonic progressions are unexpected—even startling—because many of the chords bear no relationship to each other. Among the examples that can be cited throughout the song, one particularly stands out because of its similarity to another passage that has become famous. However, in this case I hasten to add that Chausson wrote his progression first; it occurs at the end of each of the two stanzas where three unrelated chords— E-flat minor, D-flat major, and E minor—are heard in succession. One is reminded of the five chords—C major, B major, A major, F minor, and D major—that Debussy wrote in Act 2, Scene 1 of *Pelléas* to portray the widening circles on the surface of the water that result from the loss of Mélisande's ring. Each series ascends, and in each instance there is a sense of mystery and suspense.

As for the total effect of Chausson's setting of "Chanson de clown," one is impressed by the economy of means; there is no padding, there are no unnecessary notes—something that cannot be said for some of the preceding *mélodies*. The result is a simple directness. At the same time the dramatic expression is powerful and poignant.

"Chanson d'amour," second of the set, comes from *Measure for Measure*, Act 4, Scene 1, where a boy sings the gentle plaint, "Take, O take those lips away,/ That so sweetly were forsworn;/ And those eyes, the break of day,/ Lights that do mislead the morn." In sharp contrast to the first Shakespearian setting, this *mélodie* contains serious weaknesses, not the least of which is the passionate, indeed almost operatic, setting of what is essentially a sad, but certainly not desperate, text. This could be—and probably is—in response to Bouchor's over-emotional translation in which lines not found in Shakespeare are interpolated. Another feature that detracts from the song—one not previously found in any of Chausson's *mélodies*—is the immediate repetition of a section of text—here, the first two lines of the poem. Although different music is provided, the effect is to hold back the forward movement for no perceptible reason. And immediately after the repetition, the emotional temperature rises, as indicated by a generally higher vocal line and a thirty-second note fluttering figure for both hands in the upper reaches of the piano. The text at that point seems to be a violation of Shakespeare on Bouchor's part, for nowhere in the original does one find the following: "But if, in spite of everything, my sorrow touches you,/ Ah, return my kisses"; it is these added lines that call forth Chausson's intense response, one that seems too passionate and overdone.

The fluttering figure is similar to some found in various Debussy accompaniments: "Il pleure dans mon coeur" (1888); "Clair de lune" (1892); "De grève" (1892–93); and "De fleurs" (1892–93), dedicated to Mme Chausson. I cannot agree with Gallois that this "panting" style in the piano part anticipates Debussy;[47] it seems more accurate to say that such accompanimental figures were common musical property of the time and were shared by many composers.

The third *mélodie* of Op. 28, "Chanson d'Ophélie," is the shortest of the set—running to only two pages—and is a setting of Ophelia's pathetic little song in the presence of the Queen (the King enters before she is finished) after the death of Hamlet—Act 4, Scene 5. The words "He is dead and gone, lady,/ He is dead and gone;/ At his head a grass green turf,/ At his heels a stone" are among Shakespeare's simplest and most effective. Why, therefore, Bouchor felt he must expand them to "He is dead, having suffered much, Milady;/ He is gone, that is a fact," and reverse the order of the head and heels ("feet" in his translation) is a puzzle. The remainder of the passage is even more freely translated.

Chausson's setting of these moving words is a combination of recitative in the vocal line and a very thin, economical supporting accompaniment. The simplicity and directness are more subdued than in "Chanson de clown" and are in keeping with the sad truth that, at this point, Ophelia has lost her sanity—a condition that the singer must make clear by intonation and subtle nuances. In its touching expressiveness, it is one of Chausson's most nearly perfect creations.

The last number in the Shakespearian set, "Chant funèbre," was written for Soprano 1, 2 and Contralto 1, 2, with full orchestral accompaniment arranged by d'Indy from the original piano version. The text is the song in *Much Ado About Nothing*, Act 5, Scene 3: "Pardon, Goddess of the night,/ Those that slew thy virgin knight;/ For the which, with songs of woe,/ Round about her tomb they go," and so on. In $\frac{6}{4}$ meter and marked *modérément lent,* it strikes a balance between horizontal and vertical movement. For roughly the first third of the piece the orchestra and chorus perform separately, and each is given separate thematic material; the orchestra concerns itself with a horizontal figure (given below), while the chorus employs material of its own in block, chordal style. Later, the orchestral melody is subjected to alterations and fragmentations in which all of the instruments participate; the fragmentation consists mainly in the detachment of the three-note motive on the second and third beats, and the repetition of this motive on various pitches and beats. As the piece progresses, the chorus shares this material in its fragmented form besides maintaining its own chordal style; there are also some staggered entrances and pairing of parts.

Fig. 12. Chausson; *Chant funèbre,* mm. 1–2

The combination of the horizontal and vertical elements—kept separate at the beginning as if to emphasize a mutual detachment—together with the vitality achieved through simultaneously different rhythmic patterns in the orchestra and chorus, reveal a sure and masterly hand. From the expressive viewpoint, the emotional tensions build as the complications increase, then subside at the end as the complexities thin out. All in all, the comment of the critic André Hallays that this is "one of the most tragic and poignant deplorations that the thought of death has ever inspired in music"[48] may not be so extravagant as, at first glance, it appears. Of the four *Chansons de Shakespeare,* it was the latest to be completed (February 22, 1897) and thus can be expected to show a mature technique. It received its first performance April 30, 1898, by a women's chorus under the direction of Mlle Thérèse Roger.

The next set of *mélodies,* Op. 34, is entitled *Deux Poèmes de Verlaine:* "La Chanson bien douce" and "Le Chevalier malheur." Both were composed in 1898, the first in June and July and the second in November, while the Chaussons were at Glion on Lake Geneva. "La Chanson bien douce," dedicated to Chausson's eldest daughter, Étiennette, was first performed on January 27, 1900, by Jeanne Remacle. No date is available for the first hearing of "Le Chevalier malheur," which was not published until 1925 in the special issue of *La Revue Musicale* devoted to Chausson; it can be assumed that this was also performed after the composer's death. Both poems are from *Sagesse,* nos. 16 and 1 respectively.

With "La Chanson bien douce" we are very close to Debussy's musical universe, and it may prove instructive to examine certain technical features of the latter as reference points for a discussion of this *mélodie.* It is appropriate first to point out the intimate connection between the artistic ideals of Verlaine and Debussy (and by extension, Chausson). In a paragraph written by the composer Paul Dukas, Debussy's friend from their student days, we read that

> Verlaine, Mallarmé, and Laforgue used to provide us with new sounds and sonorities. They cast a light on words such as had ·never been seen before; they used methods that were unknown to the poets that had preceded them; they made their verbal material yield subtle and powerful effects hitherto undreamt of. Above all, they conceived their poetry or prose like musicians, they tended it with the care of musicians and, like musicians, too, they sought

to express their ideas in corresponding sound values. It was the writers, not the musicians, who exercised the strongest influence on Debussy. [49]

Edward Lockspeiser makes the connection more explicit in the following passage:

Some of [Verlaine's] dicta are distinctly prophetic of the creed of Debussy. "The essential task is to shorten the distance between sensation and expression," he proclaimed. Some thirty years later we find Debussy underlining the same idea: "How much there is to suppress and prune away in order to arrive at the naked flesh of feeling."

Later in the same article Lockspeiser adds:

An intimate union of word and song resulted, as Verlaine wished, less intense in emotional appeal, less picturesque perhaps than the corresponding union in the German lied, but more delicate and more poignant in expression. Not always are means and sentiment perfectly matched; sometimes a too-self-conscious attempt at delicacy results in insipidity. [50]

To effect this union in the sense of matching subtle poetic nuances with equally subtle music, Debussy employed such procedures as are recounted by Maurice Emmanuel, a fellow student of Debussy's at the Paris Conservatoire. In his little study of *Pelléas et Mélisande,* there is this description of Debussy's improvisations at the piano around 1883:

There were chains of consecutive fifths and octaves which, instead of being avoided were associated in parallel series; sevenths which, far from being discreetly "resolved downwards," led "upwards" or were not resolved at all; shameless "false relations"; chords of the ninth on all degrees of the scale; chords of the eleventh, of the thirteenth; all the notes of the diatonic scale sounded simultaneously in fantastic arrangements. [51]

Of greater value than this anecdote is Emmanuel's description, taken down verbatim in a notebook, of the conversations in 1889 between Debussy and his former composition teacher, Ernest Guiraud, on various musical topics about which Debussy had very definite convictions.[52] In Emmanuel's study of Debussy's opera, they appear in various parts of the book under such topical headings as harmony, rhythm, and vocal style. The harmonic procedures may be summarized as follows: the nonfunctional use (in the sense of correct resolutions) of chords of any one kind arranged in parallel motion; mixtures of various types of unresolved chords; incomplete chords, "reduced to seconds, thirds, fourths, and fifths, altered or not, etc., and whose uncertain tonality, precisely sought after, corresponds to complex, obscure, and unquiet thoughts or sentiments";[53] modal harmonies; and enharmonic modulations. The result of all this is, of course, tonal ambiguity. Three Debussy *mélodies* where parallel, nonfunctional chords may be seen are "De fleurs," "De rêve," and "En sourdine"; in the last there is a series of unresolved dominant sevenths.

With respect to Chausson's *mélodies,* there is evidence to suggest that in the songs of the late 1890s there is a real tendency toward tonal ambiguity. However, it is not a matter of a steady increase from song to song for, chronologically speaking, the means whereby such ambiguity is achieved are weaker in some *mélodies,* stronger in others, and lacking in still others. This situation suggests that Chausson thought of tonal ambiguity in terms of application in individual circumstances; Debussy's concept of it, on the other hand, was more likely to be in terms of an avowed policy.

As for "La Chanson bien douce," if the arpeggiated and broken chords are analyzed vertically, it will be seen that many of them are sevenths and ninths whose progression is nonfunctional. Harmonic blurring is effected in the first measures to the extent that there is little tonic feeling; in fact, the tonic is not firmly established in either voice or accompaniment until the final measures. The first eight

measures of accompaniment appear below; after the first
measure, the remaining measures are shown in chordal form
so that the progressions may be more readily seen. In a sense
these broken chords come to be accepted by the ear as ful-
filling a tonic function, for they reappear at the beginning
of the *mélodie's* final section. Exactly the same procedure is
followed in Debussy's *Les Angélus* of 1891.

Fig. 13. Chausson; *La Chanson bien douce,* mm. 1–8

As a setting of Verlaine's poem, Chausson's music matches
the gentleness and forbearance of the words, whose message
is that our mission is "to make another soul less sad," that
"our life is kindness," and "that of hate and of envy nothing
remains when death has come." The delicacy and nonfunctional vagueness of the harmonies, couched in flowing
sixteenth-note movement, as well as the thin texture, are

perfect vehicles for Verlaine's thought. The vocal line is set just as carefully; its very narrow range (a major ninth), predominantly conjunct movement, and consistent use of notes of small value in setting the equally stressed syllables of the language all contribute to the calmness, order, and understatement so typically French. In choosing this poem Chausson echoed his own basic philosophy of life— a philosophy found in many of the poems of *Sagesse,* written after Verlaine's imprisonment at Mons and his conversion to Catholicism. Whether Chausson was aware that the poet's conversion was an easygoing thing that could be—and was— easily relaxed when circumstances demanded is, perhaps, beside the point; the artist in Chausson was too busy responding to the artist in Verlaine.

"Le Chevalier malheur" is an allegorical poem in which the elements of conversion are strongly emphasized in a miraculous sort of way through the action of the evil knight. The definite imagery of the poem, in contrast to the vaporousness of "La Chanson bien douce," evokes a correspondingly definite setting from Chausson—one in which a strong tonic (C-sharp minor) is established, although at the end E major is substituted. Between these polarities many modulatory passages are found; however, the harmonies used to effect them are stronger and less tenuous than in the preceding *mélodie.* Faithfulness to poetic imagery is evident, as in the passage where the evil knight menacingly approaches to the accompaniment of a galloping figure. Surprisingly, at this late point in Chausson's career, the *Tristan* Chord is much in evidence.

It is very regrettable that Chausson set only three of the poems of Verlaine; one cannot but feel that an extended creative association would have produced *mélodies* of increasing sensitivity. As I mentioned earlier, Chausson owned a copy of *Sagesse*, and it can be assumed that he also possessed other works of Verlaine such as *La Bonne Chanson,* from which comes "Apaisement" (or "La Lune blanche"), the first of his Verlaine songs. Whether Chausson and Verlaine ever met is problematical; if they did, a close union would most likely have been impossible, for if Chausson's bourgeois respectability was scandalized by some of Debussy's antics, how much more it would have been offended by Verlaine's alcoholism and general debauchery! However, there seems to be no doubt that Chausson knew Verlaine's worth as a gifted poet, for on March 1, 1890, Léon Deschamps, editor of the literary review, *La Plume,* published the names of persons who, by their financial subscriptions, had made possible the publication of Verlaine's *Dédicaces.* Chausson was on the list, together with Mallarmé, Bouchor, Dumas *fils,* Edmond de Goncourt, Jean Richepin, Théodore de Banville, François Coppée, and others.

Op. 36 also contains two *mélodies—Cantique à l'épouse* and *Dans la forêt du charme et de l'enchantement.* The first of these, set to a poem by Albert Jounet, has no dedicatee; it was written in June 1898 and was first performed by Thérèse Roger on March 20, 1901. The poem is a love-song with—for once—no overtones of tragedy or loss, and Chausson's setting mirrors the calm tranquillity in a largely conjunct vocal line and a flowing accompaniment. The F-major tonality is strongly assertive in the first and third sections of the song, although in each instance it is tempered by unrelated chromatic harmonies in the middle that act as parenthetical expressions strengthening the tonality on either side. The middle of the *mélodie* features wide-ranging keys set in triplet figures, as opposed to the simple eighths of the first and last sections. Thus a very free ternary form results.

Dans la forêt du charme et de l'enchantement was finished at Glion on October 28, 1898—three weeks before "Le Chevalier malheur"—and was dedicated to Jeanne Remacle, by whom it was first sung, together with "La Chanson bien douce," on January 27, 1900. The poem is by Jean Moréas, one of the most dedicated of the Symbolists and the poet who first coined the term *Symbolism;* later, with Charles Maurras he founded the *École Romane* in an attempt to reestablish the classical background of French literature, thus influencing his contemporaries to write in classical idioms. Of Greek birth—originally he was Iannis Pappa-diamantopoulos—he had totally adopted French culture since his arrival in Paris in 1870. By 1881 he was one of Verlaine's fervent disciples and, together with him was a habitué of Left Bank cafés like Côte d'Or and Vachette's. Later he held forth at the last-named establishment as his fame grew; Gide and Debussy were also its frequenters. Verlaine dedicated three poems to him and mentioned him in ten others; many of these comments are uncomplimentary, because Verlaine, by his own admission, grew jealous as Moréas acquired recognition. "He was small and skinny and sickly, with black skin, black nails, and black hair, and he dressed like a music-hall swell."[54] Again, hardly a person with whom Chausson would have been on close terms, assuming they ever met.

The poem selected by Chausson is certainly of the Symbolist persuasion: golden scepters, gnomes, mirage, and deception—all a part of an enchanted forest—attest to that. Chausson's treatment of this nebulous material is not so indefinite as one might suppose, for the tonality (G minor) is clearly established before various transitions take us far from the basic key; in the final section, G minor is once more carefully asserted. This rather conventional harmonic scheme is offset, however, by rhythmic figures consisting of thirty-second notes in the right-hand part; their delicate tracery imparts a shimmering buoyancy that well expresses the charmed and enchanted surroundings. Twice in the course of the song a left-hand sixteenth-note figure under the thirty-seconds reminds one strongly of the "writing" motif that Moussorgsky used to accompany Pimen's chronicle of Russian history in Act 1 of *Boris Godunov*. There it is somber, while in Chausson's *mélodie* it is light (Figure 14). The vocal line, as is the case in so many of Chausson's later *mélodies,* pursues its own course unaided by the piano.

Fig. 14. Chausson; *Dans la forêt du charme et de l'enchantement,* mm. 13-14

Chanson Perpétuelle (Op. 37), the final *mélodie,* was finished in Paris December 17, 1898. Dedicated to the opera singer Jeanne Raunay, it was first performed by her in Le Havre on January 29, 1899, with the composer present; on the same program, the latter conducted parts of his incidental music for *La Tempête.* Daughter of the painter Jules Richomme, Mme Raunay made her operatic debut in 1888 as Uta in Ernest Reyer's *Sigurd.* In 1896 she sang Guilhen in d'Indy's *Fervaal* at the Théâtre de la Monnaie in Brussels—the opera house where Chausson's *Le Roi Arthus* was first presented in 1903. A photograph of her as Iphigénie in *Iphigénie en Tauride* of Gluck appears in Pierre Lalo's *La Musique, 1898-99.* She was a guest from time to time at 22 Boulevard de Courcelles, and in 1903 at the Schola Cantorum she sang *Chanson Perpétuelle,* "Les Heures" from *Trois Lieder,* and *Serres chaudes* at an all-Chausson concert organized by d'Indy as a memorial.

The poet of *Chanson Perpétuelle* is Charles Cros, a friend of Verlaine and accomplished in such unrelated fields as philology and science; during the 1880s he maintained a salon.[55] The poem is long and desperately sad, concerned with a woman whose lover has deserted her. Chausson's setting is scored for piano, orchestra, or a combination of piano and string quartet. The tremolo figures in portions of the accompaniment can be realized effectively only in the latter two versions.

After some of the preceding *mélodies,* with their indefinite Debussy-like harmonies, *Chanson Perpétuelle* is almost conventional. The C-sharp minor tonic is strongly affirmed in the beginning, middle, and end; modulations are made to G-sharp minor, F-sharp major, C-sharp major, and F major. The principal theme (Figure 15), present in the accompaniment only, appears in some of the above-mentioned foreign keys. The middle portion of the song is built on a triplet figure derived from the triplet in the main theme. The tremolos are reserved for the emotional climaxes in the poem: at the point where, after the kiss, the two become lovers, and later when he tires of her and she is resigned to suicide. The tremolos are also effectively used at the very end after the vocal line has concluded.

Fig. 15. Chausson; *Chanson Perpétuelle,* mm. 1–2

Chausson's final *mélodie* elicited a number of very favorable comments, among which are the following: "the most beautiful lied [*sic*] with orchestra . . . in French music";[56] "so serious, so noble and so tender with an orchestral accompaniment in which everything sighs and sings like human voices";[57] "a marvel of penetrating emotion."[58]

And so at the end of Chausson's career as a composer of

mélodies we have come full circle with respect to the type of poem found in *Nanny* and *Chanson Perpétuelle*—the bitter dregs of a love forever lost. In between these poles are many other *mélodies* of a similar type, interspersed, however, with other songs that are serene and happy—like *Sérénade italienne, Hébé, La Cigale, La Pluie,* and *Les Papillons.*

In summarizing Chausson's *mélodies,* several characteristics common to many songs should be mentioned. One of these is the consistency with which Chausson employs the flatted sixth and seventh degrees of the scale, not just as a normal progression of the melodic minor but also in association with major keys. Their appearance imparts a definite flavor wherever they are found; they are important ingredients in the overall elegiac quality so often encountered in Chausson. Among the *mélodies* containing them are *Amour d'antan, Apaisement, L'Aveu, Ballade, Cantique à l'épouse, Chanson d'Ophélie, Les Heures, Lassitude, Nocturne, Sérénade, Serre d'ennui,* and *Le Temps des lilas.*

The flatted second degree in both major and minor is also to be seen, although less often than in the case of the flatted sixths and sevenths. This is, of course, a sign of modality, but when it occurs in a diatonic context (which in Chausson's songs is practically all of the time), it stands out expressively and heightens the resigned, elegiac content. Examples of it appear in *Chanson d'Ophélie, Nanny, Printemps triste,* and *Le Temps des lilas.*

Chausson's vocal lines tend to group themselves into types, at least as far as the first few measures are concerned. By far the largest classification consists of those lines that describe a curve in the following pattern: the melody begins low and ascends scalewise and by leap to a note anywhere from a third to a sixth above the initial note before descending, sometimes scalewise or by leap, to the beginning note or to one close to it. *Mélodies* that fall into this group are *L'Aveu, Chanson Perpétuelle, La Dernière Feuille, Les Heures, Lassitude,* and *Nos Souvenirs.* Sometimes there are smaller arcs within the larger curve, as in *La Chanson bien douce*. A much smaller group employs vocal lines that begin high and descend to a note anywhere from a fourth to an octave below the starting point; the downward movement may be partially chromatic, as in *Nanny* and *Printemps triste,* or it may be a combination of diatonic movement and a slight upward bulge before the final descent, as in *Serre d'ennui.*

From a formal viewpoint, Chausson's *mélodies* are very free; most of them fall into some sort of ternary structure in which the concluding section is only a very general reminder of the initial section. Usually the harmonic scheme of the third part will duplicate that of the first for the opening measures, and the vocal line will return with the first phrase, although it is almost always changed rhythmically to conform to the text; sometimes new notes are inserted here and there. The final part of the third section is often new but within the context of the prevailing emotional climate of the first section's corresponding part. Thus by bringing back in the final section just enough of section one to reorient the listener—but in a nonliteral way—Chausson is free to exercise his inventiveness and to show us the possibilities present in the remaining text. The result is a product that is sensitive to the poem in every way, disciplined, and yet seemingly effortless, despite the enormous struggle that went on beneath the surface with respect to some of the *mélodies.*

Taking everything into account, the songs reveal a composer who, from the beginning, had an innate understanding of the *mélodie* and its problems. Chausson's solutions to these problems thrust him into the very front rank of French *mélodie* composers. To be sure, not all of his *mélodies* are equal in quality—a conclusion I have emphasized more than once—but then, neither are Fauré's, Debussy's, or Ravel's. The best of them, however, *are* equal to their best and deserve a solid and enduring place in the repertory.

NOTES

1. Denis Stevens, ed., *A History of Song* (New York: W. W. Norton and Co., Inc., 1961), p. 201.

2. Sydney Northcote, *The Songs of Henri Duparc* (London: Dennis Dobson, Ltd., 1949), pp. 73–74.

3. Ibid., p. 60.

4. Ibid., pp. 60–61.

5. Frits Noske, *French Song From Berlioz to Duparc,* trans. Rita Benton, 2d ed. rev. Rita Benton and Frits Noske (New York: Dover Publications, Inc., 1970).

6. Bainbridge Crist, *The Art of Setting Words to Music* (New York: Carl Fischer, Inc., 1944), p. 20.

7. Noske, *French Song From Berlioz to Duparc,* pp. 242–43.

8. Ibid., p. 244.

9. Ibid., p. 211.

10. Just how involved this whole question of the musical treatment of the *e muet* can become is pointed out by Noske in his previously cited work. On pp. 63–64, he gives some detailed rules on the subject from Henri Woollett, *Petit traité de prosodie à l'usage des compositeurs* (Le Havre, 1903). According to Woollett the musical factors that determine the correct usage of the *e muet* are strong and weak beats, notes of shorter or longer value, and notes of higher or lower pitch. When the various practical combinations of these factors are taken into account, the complexities of the problem can be appreciated. Noske indicates, however, that the strictness of these rules can be modified by a more flexible treatment; Woollett demands strict compliance, and even cites certain *mélodies* of Fauré and Debussy that he feels violate his precepts.

11. Gallois refers to the mode as Dorian (*Ernest Chausson,* p. 23).

12. Zuckerman, *The First Hundred Years of Wagner's Tristan,* p. 30.

13. Ibid., p. 11.

14. Donald Jay Grout, *A Short History of Opera* (New York: Columbia University Press, 1947), pp. 397–98.

15. Gerald Abraham, *A Hundred Years of Music,* 2d ed. (London: Duckworth, 1949), pp. 116–17. The complete analyses of Tovey and Dyson appear in the articles on harmony in the *Encyclopedia Britannica* and *Grove's Dictionary* respectively, that of Kurth in his *Romantische Harmonik und ihre Krise in Richard Wagners "Tristan".*

16. Band 2 der *Orpheus*–Schriftenreihe zu Grundfragen der Musik (Düsseldorf: Gesellschaft zur Förderung der systematischen Musikwissenschaft, 1962).

17. On p. 12 of *Der Tristan-Akkord,* Vogel points out the use of this chord in Beethoven's Piano Sonata in E-flat, Op. 31, no. 3, first movement, m. 36. Except for spelling, the chord is identical, even to position and spacing.

18. Zuckerman, *The First Hundred Years of Wagner's Tristan,* p. 18.

19. Ibid., p. 193. Kurth indicates many of the places in *Romantische Harmonik,* pp. 44–96.

20. Quoted in Oulmont, *Musique de l'amour,* p. 126 n.

21. Poldowski was the *nom de plume* of Irene Regine Wieniawska. Daughter

of the violinist Henri Wieniawski, she was born in Brussels in 1880 and died in London in 1932. She was known as Lady Dean Paul by virtue of her marriage to an Englishman, Sir Aubrey Dean Paul; altogether, she set twenty-one poems by Verlaine.

22. Oscar Thompson, *Debussy: Man and Artist* (New York: Tudor Publishing Co., 1940), p. 86.

23. "Ernest van Dyck," *The International Cyclopedia of Music and Musicians,* 9th ed., p. 2286.

24. G. Jean-Aubry, "A French Composer: Ernest Chausson," *The Musical Times* 59 (November 1, 1918): 500; Arthur Hoerée, "Chausson et la musique française," *La Revue Musicale,* December 1, 1925, p. 193.

25. Demuth, *César Franck,* p. 211.

26. Vallas, *Claude Debussy,* p. 59.

27. Gallois, *Ernest Chausson,* p. 42.

28. Constantin Brailoïu, "Pentatony in Debussy's Music," *Studia Memoriae Belae Bartók Sacra,* 3d ed. (London: Boosey and Hawkes, Ltd., 1959), p. 414.

29. "Lettres de Henri Duparc à Ernest Chausson," *Revue de Musicologie* 38 (December 1956):138–39.

30. W. D. Halls, *Maurice Maeterlinck: Study of His Life and Thought* (London: Oxford University Press, 1960), p. 39.

31. Barricelli and Weinstein, *Ernest Chausson,* p. 121.

32. Quoted in Oulmont, *Musique de l'amour,* p. 66.

33. Quoted in Vallas, *The Theories of Claude Debussy,* p. 47.

34. Oulmont, *Musique de l'amour,* pp. 66–67.

35. Ibid., p. 68.

36. Ibid., pp. 67–68.

37. Ibid., p. 112. See chap. 1, n. 51 for an explanation of this rather enigmatic question.

38. Gallois, *Ernest Chausson,* p. 93.

39. Cooper, *French Music,* p. 63. See chap. 1, n. 52 for a further discussion of this point.

40. Vallas, *Claude Debussy,* p. 60.

41. Lockspeiser, *Debussy: His Life and Mind,* 1:48 n.

42. Quoted in Barricelli and Weinstein, *Ernest Chausson,* p. 59.

43. Gallois, *Ernest Chausson,* p. 52.

44. Quoted in Lesure, "Claude Debussy, Ernest Chausson et Henri Lerolle," p. 340.

45. Quoted in Vallas, *Claude Debussy,* p. 55.

46. Ibid., p. 90.

47. Gallois, *Ernest Chausson,* p. 96.

48. Printed in Barricelli and Weinstein, *Ernest Chausson,* p. 129. The remark originally appeared in "Le Roi Arthus," *Revue de Paris* 6 (December 15, 1903):852.

49. Quoted in Vallas, *Claude Debussy,* p. 52.

50. Edward Lockspeiser, "The French Song in the Nineteenth Century," *The Musical Quarterly* 26 (April 1940):198–99.

51. Maurice Emmanuel, *Pelléas et Mélisande de Claude Debussy* (Paris: Libraire Delaplane, n.d.), p. 103.

52. These conversations are reproduced in Appendix B of Lockspeiser's *Debussy: His Life and Mind,* 1:204–8.

53. Emmanuel, *Pelléas et Mélisande de Claude Debussy,* p. 111.

54. Joanna Richardson, *Verlaine* (New York: The Viking Press, 1971), p. 243.

55. Further details of his life and that of his talented mistress, Nina de Callias, will be found in Richardson, *Verlaine,* pp. 17–18 and 204–5.

56. Camille Mauclair, *La Religion de la musique* (Paris: Fischbacher, 1909), p. 234. Printed in Barricelli and Weinstein, *Ernest Chausson,* p. 100. The objection to the word *lied* is mine.

57. Louis Laloy in S.I.M., (August–September, 1910). Printed in Barricelli and Weinstein, *Ernest Chausson,* p. 100.

58. Henri Gauthier-Villars, eulogy for Chausson (June 19, 1899) in *Garcon, l'Audition!* Printed in Barricelli and Weinstein, *Ernest Chausson,* p. 107.

── 3 ──

Music For Orchestra

CHAUSSON'S first venture into the orchestral field was
the composition of the first of his symphonic poems,
Viviane, Op. 5, written in 1882 and dedicated to Jeanne
Escudier, the young lady who was to become Mme Chausson
the following year. Despite its low opus number and the
fact that Chausson at the time was studying composition
under Franck, *Viviane* is a solid achievement and deserves
a place in today's repertory. As a symphonic poem it com-
pares very favorably with other French examples of this
non-French genre—works like Franck's *Les Éolides, Le
Chasseur maudit, Les Djinns;* Duparc's *Lenore*; and Saint-
Saëns's four pieces; in actuality it is superior to some of those
named. In listening to it carefully, one gets the impression
that the composer allows the underlying story to unfold
more naturally in the illustrative music; in other words, he
does not appear to work so hard or so self-consciously to
find the music that vividly describes the scene, whereas
Franck in *Le Chasseur maudit* and Duparc in *Lenore* seem
labored.

For his background, Chausson dipped into the Arthurian
legends, specifically that part which concerns the magician
Merlin and his mistress, Viviane. On the score's title page
the composer has indicated the four divisions of the work:
"Viviane et Merlin dans la Forêt de Brocéliande; Scène
d'Amour; Les envoyés du Roi Arthur parcourent la forêt à
la recherche de l'Enchanteur. Il veut fuir et les rejoindre;

Viviane endort Merlin et l'entoure d'aubépines en fleurs."
It seems that Merlin in a weak moment had revealed one
of his spells to his paramour, and she turned the tables and
used it on him by putting him to sleep.

So subtly are the sections put together that the music's
flow remains undisturbed. Offstage trumpet calls interrupt
the gently pulsating *scène d'amour*; a gathering tension and
excitement portray Merlin's attempts to escape Viviane's
clutches; while a highly original cadenzalike passage for
harp, embedded in the surrounding orchestration, depicts
Viviane's ensnaring tactics. Mellow horn passages serve as
a unifying factor by suggesting the forest setting. Here and
there a chromatic passage and the *Tristan* Chord inevitably
suggest Wagner, but these are minor points in an altogether
charming and rewarding score. The work was first heard
March 31, 1883, at the Société Nationale under Colonne's
direction; after some revisions Lamoureux performed it on
January 29, 1888. In January 1899 it was heard in Moscow,
where an American critic spoke very favorably of it. It did
not fare so well at a Parisian performance in 1884 when
Duvernoy, the critic of *République Française*, informed his
readers that "it is with pain that we have followed the
numerous movements indicated on the program." After
acknowledging that the work has a certain talent in it, he
went on to say that certain Wagnerian procedures could be
found.[1]

Chausson's second symphonic poem,[2] *Soir de fête*, is a
late work, having been written in 1897-98 at Fiesole; desig-
nated as Op. 32, it was first performed March 13, 1898 by
Colonne, to whom it was dedicated. In a letter of October
1898 to Octave Maus, Chausson set forth his objectives in
composing it: "I simply wanted to note down a personal
impression of the distant noise of a crowd; as contrast, the
calm and serene night. The difficulty lay in the transposition.
To give the idea of a joyful throng without employing any

of those rhythms and phrases which seem to be obligatory in characterizing a celebration."[3]

The work is not one of Chausson's successes, despite the thought and effort that obviously went into it. For one thing, its thematic material is undistinguished and commonplace. Gallois mentions its "rather dull" orchestration and goes on to say that the "enthusiasm" and the "youth" found in *Viviane* are lacking.[4] Certainly the spontaneity and effortlessness that are so impressive in the earlier work are totally missing. The very vagueness of Chausson's poetic conception gave rise to a corresponding vagueness in structure as well as to music that lacks sharpness of outline. One feels that the composer's aspirations outpaced his abilities to realize his objectives. Such a poetic conception requires more daring than Chausson possessed, also a less inhibited nature—qualities amply demonstrated by Debussy's brilliant juxtaposition of "Les parfums de la nuit" and "Le matin d'un jour de fête" in his *Ibéria*. Perhaps the public's instinctive awareness of such lacks accounted for the cold reception accorded *Soir de fête* at its premiere. The critics followed suit, the Belgian correspondent of *Soir* remarking that the work "commends itself by clever instrumental workmanship rather than by originality; the character of a festival, more especially of a popular festival, is totally missing: it is not at all joyful. After all, there are festivals where one does not enjoy oneself. Perhaps that is what the composer wished to express."[5] Most likely, Chausson's aversion to using "any of those rhythms and phrases" that immediately suggest a "celebration" is the culprit here, for the absence of such devices created an ambiguity that the public no doubt perceived. In trying too hard not to be obvious, Chausson failed where he could have succeeded had he handled the old clichés in a new way; the result would have been more natural and less forced.

By far the most important orchestral work of Chausson's career is his Symphony in B-flat major, Op. 20, composed in 1889-90 and dedicated to his brother-in-law, Henri Lerolle. The present treatment and discussion of this work take into account the rather unpleasant fact that outward circumstances and unfavorable—even hostile and irresponsible—criticisms have constantly forced comparisons between it and Franck's Symphony in D minor. I shall thus approach Chausson's symphony from this angle, comparing it to Franck's symphony in terms of structure, thematic material, instrumentation and the like; only in this way can the misconceptions be corrected. It will then be seen that Chausson's symphony, although undeniably a product of the Franck school, can and does stand alone as an original and powerful contribution to the French symphonic repertory.

The external circumstances alluded to above concern the Franckists, whose unabashed hero-worship of their mentor led them to compose works that, at least superficially, certainly seem derivative and, in fact, often are. But the critics of the time over-reacted and, in a number of instances, completely failed to acknowledge the original details that set works of master and pupils apart. Some of the fault for this failure can certainly be assigned to the Franckists themselves, for public diplomacy and tact in defense of Franck were never strong points with them and, as mentioned earlier, human nature tended to take over as the critics punished all of the Franckists for their belligerency and indiscretion. As one of the leaders of the group, Chausson felt their cold wrath frequently; so often, in fact, that one must admire his dogged determination to proceed in the face of overwhelming odds.

Today's criticisms, while somewhat more fair and objective, still contain passages that place Chausson in an adverse positon with respect to Franck. One such criticism, written by Norman Demuth, points out that Chausson's symphony falls upon the similar work of Franck for its framework and construction. Further, when Franck has a choral, then Chausson must have one as well. It sounds as if Franck had for a moment returned to the happiness of *Les Éolides* and *Psyché*, indeed, the unbelievers have been known to refer to it as "Franck No. 2."

The workmanship is fine and the orchestral touch much more varied in its application than that of Franck, for Chausson knew and talked with d'Indy, who was a master of orchestration and orchestral instruments.[6]

Another modern point of view in the same vein is that of Martin Cooper:

> The opening chorale inevitably suggests Franck, but it it is not until the last movement that Chausson's music becomes simply reminiscent. There the whole lay-out of the movement and the nature of the material is so like that of the last movement (also the weakest) of Franck's symphony that it seems as though the imitation must have been conscious.[7]

If we consider the similarities in "framework and construction" first, it is obvious that both symphonies are in three movements and that each is constructed on the cyclical principle, although Chausson's is less rigorous in the application of this principle than is Franck's. Whereas Franck in his last movement reintroduces the principal theme of his second movement in both development and recapitulation (both third movements are in sonata form), and brings back the first and third themes of his first movement in the coda, Chausson interrupts the flow of his sonata form only once—in the coda—by restating the introductory theme of his first movement. Thus, the ground plans of the two last movements are really quite different. Even if they were similar, it seems as odd to point out the resemblances in a fault-finding kind of way as it would be to criticize Beethoven for employing the sonata form he inherited from Haydn and Mozart; to my knowledge, no one has yet done that! And just as Beethoven altered certain details of sonata form to suit his requirements, so the followers of Franck changed the face of cyclical form to meet their needs. Alterations in basic construction are, after all is said and done, ways by means of which art forms move forward in their accommodations to new or expanded content.

There are other noticeable differences in formal structure: the material of Chausson's slow introduction appears in altered form in the development section of the following *allegro,* but it is not used as the basis for either of the principal themes of that movement. In this respect it differs from Franck's treatment, for the latter's slow introduction is followed by an *allegro* whose main theme is derived from it. Another difference is that Franck's introduction and immediately following exposition are presented twice—first in D minor and the second time in F minor. Thus a double exposition results in which the introductory material is employed as an organic, structural feature having thematic significance. Donald Tovey is quick to point out a precedent for this:

> When we see César Franck twice alternating his introduction with his allegro, we instantly recognize the influence of Beethoven's B-flat Quartet, Op. 130; and so, in all probability, did Franck himself.[8]

The second movements of the symphonies are also outwardly dissimilar; where Franck injects *scherzo* elements into a predominantly slow movement, Chausson maintains a solemn *adagio* throughout. Two similarities belonging on a more localized level are the assignment of important themes to the English horn in both movements, and the *fortissimo* canonic treatment by opposing masses of instruments in Chausson's second movement and in Franck's first. There are subtle differences, however, for Chausson's English horn passage is doubled by the solo violoncello (measures 46–54), while Franck's is heard alone (measures 16–32), although later it is doubled by the bass clarinet. And Franck's canonic passage concerns his main first-movement theme and is absolutely strict (measures 513–16), while Chausson's is involved with transitional material leading to a restatement of his principal second-movement theme, breaking off into free imitation in the second measure (measures 72–74) as a result of changed intervallic relationships.

As for orchestration, with the exception of minor differences the instrumentation of the two symphonies is essentially the same. Franck's orchestra is slightly smaller and more conventional, requiring in all three movements only two flutes, two bassoons, and two trumpets; whereas Chausson requires three flutes, three bassoons, and four trumpets. The difference in the two scores is reduced somewhat in that Franck calls for two cornets in addition to his trumpets in his first and final movements.

With respect to Chausson's orchestration, Demuth's estimate of the latter's "orchestral touch" as being "much more varied" is entirely correct. Chausson provides more solo passages than Franck, especially in his first and last movements; and there is throughout his symphony a greater emphasis on individual choirs, the woodwinds particularly achieving a group independence that Franck does not give them. The same is true of the brass, which functions as a unit in Chausson's presentation of his chorale theme in the development section of his first movement, and also in the coda of the *finale.* Chausson also distributes small melodic figures among various instruments to a greater degree than Franck, thus achieving more variety in orchestral colors.

One point that can hardly fail to impress itself upon the attentive listener is a certain dichotomy of styles in Chausson's symphony. The introduction to the first movement, and most of the second movement, while unrelated thematically to anything in the D minor symphony, are closely allied with Franck's motivic construction, short-breathed phrases, and harmonic chromaticism. On the other hand, the first-movement *allegro* is free of these influences, while the last movement falls somewhere between these extremes. Yet even in the midst of the similarities, large differences in the handling of details reveal two quite distinctive musical minds at work. These are matters that require a rather close examination.

The raw materials of the vast majority of Franck's music, be it orchestral, organ, piano, or chamber, are essentially the same: melodies whose basic phrase unit is generally four measures, with frequent subdivisions into two-measure units—the short-breathed phrases mentioned above. The two-measure phrases—as well as the often-found one-measure units—are made up of motivic, cellular members of the total four-or eight-measure theme. Because so many of these motivic members were initially intended to assume important functions in chromatically conceived transitions and modulations—Franck's basic harmonic style—their careful separation into short units is noticeable even to the average listener. As they begin to fulfill their transitional and modulatory functions by being subtly altered or employed in strict sequential patterns, one begins to question what the ultimate harmonic goal is, as key after key is traversed in the course of the journey. Such puzzlement is implicit in Ambroise Thomas's acid query when he criticized Franck's symphony:

> How can it be called a symphony in D minor when the first theme at the ninth measure goes into D-flat, at the tenth into C-flat, at the twenty-first into F-sharp minor, at the twenty-fifth into B-flat minor, at the twenty-sixth into C minor, at the thirty-ninth into E-flat major, at the forty-ninth into F minor?[9]

Thomas was, of course, the ultra-conservative director of the Paris Conservatoire, and was confusing "transitions" with "modulations." The only real modulation in Thomas's observations is the change last mentioned, for it is at this point that Franck begins his reexposition in F minor. Everything up to that point must be considered as momentary transitions *through* the enumerated keys en route from D minor to F minor, the two polarities that govern Franck's expositions.

Franck himself, of course, was always aware of his overall harmonic plans, and he communicated his convictions in this important area to his pupils when, in September 1884, he wrote to Pierre de Bréville, "Your tonality must *never* be in any way doubtful."[10] Léon Vallas emphasizes Franck's harmonic sense by saying that

> one of [his] natural endowments was an overriding sense of tonality, which gave him scope to reinforce the solidity of structures already well founded. Despite the incessant ambiguity of his style, with its subtle gradations of tonality, an inflexible discipline controls the tonal waywardness and directs it towards the realization of the composer's basic plan with its finely balanced design.[11]

Because Franck's sense of direction toward definite tonal goals is so strong, his materials are fashioned to serve the larger purpose of making those goals and the routes whereby they are reached absolutely clear; therefore, the more directly, economically, and free from unnecessary ornamentation his melodic and rhythmic matter can be constructed, the more easily he can attain his objective. The result, of course, is an astonishingly compressed style.

It is when Chausson employs the same sort of short-breathed motivic material that similarities to the Franck style occur; but closer examination will show that his more relaxed and expansive handling of details renders some of the likenesses superficial. A good illustration occurs when, after Chausson and Franck have unveiled the melodies with which their introductions open (Figure 16), each composer submits motivic fragments to sequential treatment (it should be observed that Chausson's theme is longer-breathed and not so readily divisible into motives as Franck's). Chausson's

Fig. 16. Chausson; Symphony, 1, mm. 1–8
Franck; Symphony, 1, mm. 1–6

sequence (Figure 17) appears as though it were organized into three two-measure segments with the second and third as exact duplicates of the first. However, measures 1, 3, and 5 (in the present example) are unlike and, of measures 2, 4, and 6, only the fourth and sixth begin the same, while differing in subsequent details. On the other hand, Franck's

Fig. 17. Chausson; Symphony, 1, mm. 25–30

sequence (Figure 18) consists of absolutely literal chromatic reproductions of the original pattern; but more important, the pattern is compressed into one measure, imparting a bare-boned tautness to the passage. Such construction is typical of Franck. On the extremely few occasions when Chausson organizes his material in the same way, the simi-

Fig. 18. Franck; Symphony, 1, mm. 25–28

larity is startling; Figure 19 provides an example from his second movement, whose main theme (Figure 20) is organized into short, Franck-like motives—precisely why the first

Fig. 19. Chausson; Symphony, 2, mm. 79–80

Fig. 20. Chausson; Symphony, 2, mm. 1–6

and last sections of this ternary movement remind one of
Franck. The lyrical middle section with its English horn
solo in B-flat minor (the same solo instrument and key
chosen by Franck for his second movement) contains padding and filler material unlike Franck. Fleeting Wagnerian
references, consisting mainly of the *Tristan* Chord, may also
be heard.

Chausson's nondependence on Franck comes to the fore
in the main *allegro* portion of his first movement. True, the
exuberant, syncopated first theme reminds one of the principal theme not of Franck's first but of his last movement
(Figure 21); however, here all similarities cease, for Chaus-

Fig. 21. Chausson; Symphony, 1, mm. 48–63
Franck; Symphony, 3, mm. 7–18

son's development section—one of the true tests of any symphonic composer's architectonic skills—bears no resemblance to the corresponding sections of either of the first or last movements of Franck's symphony.

A detailed comparison of each composer's first-movement development reveals Franck's carefully systematized tonal plan, operating almost ruthlessly according to formula, as opposed to Chausson's more relaxed, even casual, manner. Franck, in 132 measures, touches on twenty-six keys, of which fifteen are different; some are more important than others, serving as landmarks or structural members of Franck's tonal thought. Of course, the melodic and rhythmic materials, and their harmonic treatment, must be of the utmost economy so that there may be order and clarity amid the almost constant transitions and modulations. The entire harmonic process of Franck's development is set out below.

The keys in which Franck remains for approximately six measures or more are those he stresses as being the important guideposts along his tonal route from exposition to recapitulation; they are the ones he is "in." Between these are others that occupy one or two measures and act as less important links in the total chain; they are the ones he is "on." There are also other measures that are strictly transitional and that contain elements of two keys. Nearly all of the keys are a major or minor third apart, although some are a major second apart; most of the latter are in descending order and are approximately in the middle of the development section. Franck's standard method of movement from one key to the next is most frequently that of chromaticism, the melodic chromaticism of the individual parts combining to form the harmonic chromaticism of the whole. As might be expected, much of this movement is sequential. However, the compression of the entire development is so great that not all of the sequential writing is complete, for some of it lacks a second transposition. Again, as might be expected, all transpositions are either harmonically exact or so close to the original harmony that no essential difference is felt. A typical example of this chromatic writing in a sequential passage, seen in measures 249–52, is reproduced in Figure 22; the passage is

Fig. 22. Franck; Symphony, 1, mm. 249–52

from that middle section of Franck's development mentioned above as consisting of keys that descend by major seconds (enharmonic equivalents in this instance). These keys, occupying two measures each, are transitional and pass to E minor which takes up six measures and is one of Franck's structural members. At the end of these six measures, the sequential passage of the illustration is repeated, the keys being E major and D major (instead of D minor); these pass to C minor which, in turn, moves quickly to A-flat major. The sequential writing is so highly organized that the two shorter sequential passages illustrated above may be considered either as independent sequences or, together with their culminations in E minor and C minor respectively, as a two-membered larger sequence. The following diagram may serve to clarify these relationships:

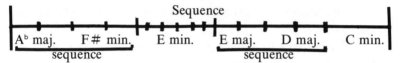

Nothing remotely approaching Franck's overall tonal architecture appears in Chausson's development, which is primarily concerned with the unfolding of melodic material. This can be observed shortly after the beginning of the development, when Chausson repeats a theme (actually, a transitional passage between the first and second themes of the exposition; except for the A on which it resolves, it is "black-note" pentatonic) several times in melodic—not harmonic—sequence before lopping off portions of it, leaving a variant of its second measure as accompanimental material. Later, the first measure of this melody serves as an ostinato accompaniment to the main theme of the introduction. And, just as in Franck's development, so in Chausson's there is a long succession and wide variety of keys; however, whereas Franck's method of entering, remaining in, and leaving keys amounts to a formula, Chausson's procedure is more flexible. He generally remains for eight measures in keys where melodic material is being emphasized, while the length of time he remains in less important and transitional keys varies from two to six measures. As a consequence, the harmonic rhythm is irregular and unpredictable, the opposite of the situation in Franck where main structural keys are often preceded and followed by balanced sequential phrases of the same length.

Chausson's transitions and modulations are also varied, and his use of complete and incomplete sequences to effect change is negligible. When sequences are employed, they are often inexact, owing to altered melodic intervals, to the redistribution of material to a lower range where it is assigned to instruments other than those which first presented it, and to a postponement of harmonic resolution. Sometimes melodic sequences over pedal points or freely-moving basses will be found.

With respect to the final movement of each symphony, Cooper's remarks concerning similarities in the nature of the material possibly referred to the recurring short phrases in the middle of each main theme, and to the long notes that constitute each of the second themes. Certainly the short phrases do suggest sequential treatment in each case, and neither composer disappoints us. One passage in Chausson that never fails to startle occurs in measures 208–14, where there is a striking resemblance to measures 364–70 not of Franck's last movement but of his first (Figure 23). Close scrutiny reveals differences, but not enough to dispel the impression that Franck's downward-plunging melodic line with its insistent rhythm lay somewhere at the back of Chausson's mind.

It is useless to speculate as to why this passage should suddenly appear in Chausson's otherwise nonderivative writing in this third movement, but one cannot but think that its unexpected appearance formed a part of the crisis that overwhelmed the composer as he struggled with his finale. In chapter 1, I quoted from a lengthy letter to Paul Poujaud in which Chausson poured out his utter frustration in connection with this last movement. A few lines later in the same letter, he wrote, "In my lucid moments I try to recognize my malady. And I have found it, all of a sudden. It comes from my songs. Ah! I detest them now and I hope never to write any again. All of them bad, except *Hébé* perhaps and fifteen measures of *Nanny*." [12]

In another and more significant letter concerning the Symphony—this one to Henri Lerolle—Chausson remarked: "I dare not think of the finale which I shall never get out of the way; I still have quite a few nice days of torture ahead of me. That is especially due to the *nature of ideas which do not lend themselves to symphonic developments*" (italics added). [13] It seems not wholly improbable that Chausson was so des-

Fig. 23. Chausson: Symphony, 3, mm. 208–14
Franck; Symphony, 1, mm. 364–70

perate at this juncture that he took the line of least resistance in trying to solve his problems, and employed a Franck-like solution to overcome his temporary paralysis.

It is appropriate at this time in assessing Chausson's Symphony to ask some questions regarding symphonic development that may be embarrassing—not to Chausson but to Franck—with a view toward comparisons in this vital area. It seems indisputable that Beethoven is the culmination and ultimate reference point as far as development sections are concerned; and rightly or wrongly, all post-Beethoven developments are judged with his supreme examples in mind. D'Indy, with all the best intentions in the world and thinking he was elevating Franck to the highest level, mentions Beethoven and his adored master in the same breath often enough to force comparisons not particularly favorable to Franck. Therefore, we must question whether the constant, formula-ridden, modulatory process carried out in the first movement of Franck's symphony, however exciting, is legitimate development. One suspects not, for themes and portions of themes are not subtly changed or used simultaneously with other fragments in a new synthesis. They are, for the most part, transposed bodily and presented again and again in the manner already described—as units in an ongoing and relentless tonal scheme. We can certainly admire and perhaps be somewhat awed by the systematic and orderly mind that produced such careful organization, but in the last analysis the whole process seems mechanical and rigid, not to say lacking in imagination. Franck even applied the same standards and rigid order to his celebrated improvisations at the Ste Clothilde organ. He used to sit quietly for a few minutes, hands on forehead and deep in thought, before beginning his long and involved tonal journeys. And is it not a bit disillusioning to learn that he constantly admonished his pupils, "when in doubt, modulate!"[14] as though the introduction of new keys was a panacea for all ills?

In comparison, it would appear that Chausson, for all his

agonizing doubts, came closer than Franck to the true nature of development when, as reported above, he dissected themes and used parts of them as accompanimental material beneath other themes. Not possessing Franck's analytical mind, his entire approach—whether he wished it to be so or not—is looser. But as a result his symphony is less densely packed, less rigid, and, as a consequence, lighter, more flowing, more rhapsodic, and, most important, more spontaneous. It is, of course, an uneven work, but it all comes together in performance and it does "sound." One suspects that with this symphony behind him, Chausson's second work in this form might have benefited from the previous experience; unfortunately, the sketches for this second essay (1899) are too incomplete for anyone to judge.

Chausson's Symphony received wide exposure during its composer's lifetime. It was first heard on April 18, 1891, at the Société Nationale, with Chausson conducting; in 1892 it was performed at the same place; Brussels heard it in 1895; Barcelona on October 31, 1896, at the Teatro Lirico, with Chausson on the podium; and its perhaps "official" Parisian performance by the Berlin Philharmonic under the direction of Arthur Nikisch on May 13, 1897—"official" because "Lamoureux had ignored it while Colonne considered it too difficult for his orchestra";[15] the Société Nationale concerts were too parochial and oriented toward the despised Franckists to be always taken seriously! Its first French performance outside of Paris occurred in Bordeaux in 1897, while the same year saw a Russian reading.

Critical opinions were mixed, and ranged from the generally enthusiastic to the openly hostile. Even better from the Franckists' point of view were some that demonstrated a shift from previous hostility or indifference to a new understanding, and furthermore were honest enough to acknowledge the change. Excerpts from two such criticisms follow: "M. Chausson, whom we had known until now as an imponderable musician, has been transformed and appears this time clear and straight-forward in his ideas" (*Figaro*); "I was all the more glad to hear and to applaud this symphony as it has happened many times that I did not at all enjoy the musical productions of the young composer, too indecisive until now in my opinion; today I believe I saw a personality asserting itself, more conscious, clearer and also more color-ful. At any rate, it is a significant work, great and beautiful in appearance which does honor to our school" (A. Ernst in *Siècle Progrès Libéral*). From the hostile side I cull the following: after a very brief setting-forth of the musical events of the first part of the first movement, the critic writ-ing in *Gazette de France* tells us, "but here it becomes so con-fused that I understood nothing. . . . If M. Chausson will but moderate himself, he will give us nice things, for he is not short of wind. But he really had too many friends in the hall; their ovations were noisy and immoderate."[17] This last sen-tence is a perfect record of the manner in which the Franck-ists annoyed the critics; it would be interesting to learn how many reviews were prejudiced by such undiplomatic be-havior. However, one more unfavorable opinion outdoes the others in its absurdity and must have caused Chausson some puzzlement, consternation, and even amusement: the day after the Berlin Philharmonic's performance of the Symphony, a M. Torchet, writing in *L'Evénement,* referred to Chausson as "a difficult author, the Mallarmé of music."[18]

The final work in Chausson's pitifully small orchestral output is his extremely popular *Poème,* Op. 25, for violin and orchestra. Of all his major works, it seems to have given him the least trouble, for it was begun in mid-April 1896 and finished not quite three months later on June 29. Dedicated to the great Belgian violinist Eugène Ysaÿe—a close friend of the composer's—*Poème* was first performed by him in Nancy on December 27, 1896, followed by its Paris debut at the Concerts Colonne, April 4, 1897, where Ysaÿe again was the soloist. It was at the latter concert that Chausson, listen-ing backstage with Camille Mauclair, expressed his incredulity at the applause following the performance.[19] On June 17, 1899, one week to the day following Chausson's death, Ysaÿe played the work in London—a performance that Chausson had planned to attend. A moving tribute was penned by Ysaÿe after the concert and addressed to Chausson's children. In part, it reads: ". . . and I, who was among the first to understand, love, and admire the intimate musician, the sincere and gently melancholic poet he was—I was today still more moved at the thought that I was the first after his death to place humbly all my artistic strength at the service of one of his works, whose pure beauty will reflect itself on all of you."[20]

Actually, *Poème* received a private performance before its public debut at Nancy, in surroundings and under conditions that make fascinating reading. Sometime in October 1896 Chausson went to Spain where, on the 31st in Barcelona—as we have seen—he conducted the Spanish premiere of his Symphony. Mathieu Crickboom, the eminent violinist, had been appointed conductor of the Catalan Society Orchestra and had enlisted the aid of both Chausson and Ysaÿe in launching his first season. The concerts of November 5 and 8 featured Ysaÿe in the Beethoven and Mendelssohn violin concerti, as well as in Bach's Chaconne in D minor. Both occasions—Ysaÿe's first appearances on Spanish soil—were resounding triumphs.[21]

Gallois's narrative continues by telling us that, by way of celebrating these successes and in order to enjoy a short diversion, Crickboom took the Chaussons and Ysaÿes to the home of his friend the Catalan painter Santiago Rusinal, at Sitgès, overlooking the Mediterranean. They were accompanied by the violinist Angenot; the cellist Gillet; Guidé, oboeist and professor at the Brussels Conservatoire; and the Spanish composers Morera and Granados.

All day, for ten hours without interrruption except for some moments at dinner, music resounded in the painter's house. Madame Chausson or Granados took turns accompanying the indefatigable Ysaÿe who, suddenly, wished to sight-read *Poème.* Towards evening, the two Spanish musicians interpreted some of their works. . . . At this moment, one may read in "La Vanguardia" of Barcelona, which gives the account of this astonishing evening, of the numerous residents of the little town—among whom were many fishermen—silently entering, and with care, passing unobserved into the recesses of the room. It was a lovely sight to see these rough men with sunburned features visibly moved by these floods of unfamiliar harmony and transported with joy; they applauded madly, asking again for the same thing three and four times! The spontaneity and sincerity of these displays kept on growing until dawn when the concert was ended. Ysaÿe found himself suddenly lifted up by the strong arms of the seamen and carried in triumph![22]

Another heartwarming experience in connection with *Poème* occurred when the Spanish composer Albeniz, who had arrived in Paris friendless in 1893 and whom Chausson had introduced to Fauré, d'Indy, Dukas, and Bordes at 22 Boulevard de Courcelles where he was a frequent guest, returned Chausson's kindness by making arrangements with Breitkopf & Haertel for *Poème's* publication. Unknown to Chausson, he paid a substantial amount from his own resources because the publishing house was unwilling to take the financial risk, feeling that the work's modernity would inhibit sales.

It seems now established that *Poème* has definite programmatic connotations. The subtitle in the upper left-hand corner of Chausson's manuscript, as photographed by Gallois and included as one of the plates in his book,[23] reads "Le Chant de l'amour triomphant"; the work's principal title, "Poème symphonique pour violon et orchestre, Op. 25," appears at the top center. The subtitle is the name of a short story by Turgenev[24]—one of Chausson's favorite authors and one whose complete works graced his spacious library.

Chausson subsequently suppressed the subtitle and dropped the word *symphonique;* finally, he decided to call it simply *Poème, Op. 25.* Gallois, following an outline of the story,[25] suggests connections between certain themes and the story's main characters; there is no way of knowing how valid or accurate these connections are, and Gallois indicates the tenuousness of such theorizing by placing question marks in appropriate spots.[26] Running through Turgenev's tale, like an *idée fixe,* is the "chant de l'amour," set to a very distinctive melody; Chausson may have considered this element of the story when he composed the first theme of his piece.

From the standpoint of formal design, *Poème* is one of its composer's most carefully constructed scores. Of its five sections, the first, third, and fifth are alike in meter ($\frac{3}{4}$), tempo (lento), and thematic material. Sections two and four in $\frac{6}{8}$ meter and marked *animato* and *allegro* respectively share the work's second principal theme. Although the sectional design of *Poème* is symmetrical, the lengths of the corresponding sections are unequal, for sections one, three, and five contain 96, 42, and 47 measures respectively; while section two has 101 as compared with section four's 61 measures.

The two principal themes are admirably contrasted. The one with which sections one, three, and five are concerned is restrained, reserved, and beautifully balanced in terms of contour. Figure 24 shows it in its first statement for unaccompanied violin; it is preceded by thirty-three measures of darkly-tinted orchestral introduction. Immediately following the violin's statement, the orchestra alone sounds the theme *pianissimo* in its simple harmonization. Exactly the same chord structure is repeated in the final section, *fortissimo,* with the violin proclaiming the second half of the melody an octave higher. Substantially the same harmonies are heard in the third section, except that instead of E-flat minor, the key is G-flat minor (the signature is G-flat major but with

Fig. 24. Chausson; *Poème,* mm. 33–47

the flatted third, the same situation as in the other sections where the key is really E-flat major with its lowered third). In all instances, Chausson's use of the flatted sixth and seventh degrees—employed in so many of his *mélodies*—imparts the same elegiac characteristic that we have seen so many times in the songs. A rhapsodic version of this first theme, played by the solo violin with much double-stopping, leads into the second section (*animato*).

Both of the fast $\frac{6}{8}$ sections are violin-dominated and are as tragically intense as the other sections are serious and reserved. However, although they share the same lyrically passionate theme, this melody is not presented in its final form until the fourth section; this gradual unfolding process is one of the characteristics of the Franck school and is found in a number of other Chausson works. Here a large part of the second section is taken up with extremely rhapsodic material out of which the first and incomplete version of the second theme is formed. Figure 25 shows the fully formed version as it appears in the fourth section.

It does not seem inappropriate to point out a family resemblance between this theme and two of Franck's best-known

Fig. 25. Chausson; *Poème,* mm. 255–58

melodies: one from the first movement of the Piano Quintet in F minor, the other from the third movement of the Sonata in A major for Violin and Piano. The two most obvious reference points are the four-measure construction of Chausson's theme with its two-measure segments, and the falling fourth from A through E in the last two measures, which recalls the similar figure at the conclusion of each Franck theme. Perhaps another circumstance that enhances the family relationship is the fact that both of the Franck works and *Poème* are among their composers' most impassioned, lyrical, and deeply emotional creations.

It is almost inconceivable how such a well-written and spontaneous-sounding work, one so enthusiastically championed by one of the greatest violinists of the time, could have been so shabbily treated in the press. Torchet, in *L'Evénement,* was in his usual, mindless form when he wrote: ". . . despite the swooning of the young and old aesthetes, I persist in thinking that it is music such as should not be written, useless, even harmful music, because, in spite of the composer's talent, it contains not an idea and fills us with great boredom."[27] In *Gil Blas,* G. Salvayre informed his readers that "as for the so-called poem by M. Ernest Chausson, it is one of the most tedious samples of the great 'school of stew without meat' that I have heard. It is pretentiously sterile and empty. I deplore sincerely that an artist of M. Ysaÿe's stature, who has so many beautiful things to play for us, should besmirch himself with such unwholesome music (if that can still be called music). . . ."[28] Time has, of course, reversed these judgments, for today *Poéme* is one of the most popular and best-loved shorter compositions in the entire repertory of the violin.

NOTES

1. Quoted in Gallois, *Ernest Chausson,* p. 135 n.

2. Actually the third, if one counts *Solitude dans les bois,* Op. 10, composed in 1886 and performed on December 12 of that year. "Chausson thought of it as 'a poem which I make up alone in my head and of which I only give a general impression to the public. . . . There is no description in it, no hint of a story; only feelings.' " Barricelli and Weinstein, *Ernest Chausson,* p. 161. For some reason, Chausson was dissatisfied with the work and destroyed it.

3. Ibid., pp. 161–62.

4. Gallois, *Ernest Chausson,* p. 136.

5. Ibid., p. 137.

6. Demuth, *César Franck,* p. 191.

7. Cooper, *French Music,* p. 65.

8. Donald Francis Tovey, *Essays in Musical Analysis* (London: Oxford University Press, 1935), 2:62.

9. Quoted in Maurice Emmanuel, *César Franck* (Paris: Librairie Renouard, 1930), p. 93.

10. Pierre de Bréville, "Les Fioretti du Père Franck," *Mercure de France* 262 (September 1, 1935):255.

11. Vallas, *César Franck,* p. 270.

12. Quoted in Barricelli and Weinstein, *Ernest Chausson,* p. 44.

13. Ibid., p. 42. Letter of 1889 to Lerolle.

14. And yet, such advice was beneficial for Franck's organ students, a group to whom it would have applied more readily than to his composition class. The former, slowly mastering the intricacies of improvisational techniques, often needed guidance as to how to proceed when they discovered that remaining in a particular key for too long a period tended to make their efforts static and dull. Modulation, as long as it is not excessive, is one way of overcoming the problem.

15. Barricelli and Weinstein, *Ernest Chausson,* p. 81.

16. Printed in Barricelli and Weinstein, *Ernest Chausson,* pp. 47–48.

17. Ibid., p. 48.

18. Quoted in Gallois, *Ernest Chausson,* p. 179.

19. See chap. 1.

20. Quoted in Barricelli and Weinstein, *Ernest Chausson,* p. 106.

21. Gallois, *Ernest Chausson,* pp. 59–60.

22. Ibid., pp. 60–61.

23. Between pp. 96–97.

24. The complete story in translation appears in *Great Russian Short Stories,* ed. Stephen Graham (New York: Liveright Publishing Corp., 1959), pp. 144–69.

25. Gallois, *Ernest Chausson,* pp. 145–46.

26. Ibid., p. 147.

27. Quoted in Barricelli and Weinstein, *Ernest Chausson,* p. 87.

28. Ibid., pp. 87–88.

———— 4 ————

Keyboard Music

I N view of the frequently imaginative, poetic, and technically skillful writing for the piano that distinguishes
many of the *mélodie* accompaniments, it is very regrettable
that Chausson wrote so little solo music for that instrument.
The reasons for this dearth are puzzling, for the piano had
occupied the composer's attention very early in his career.
In April 1878 there was a Sonatina in G minor followed in
January 1879 by a second one in D minor; both of these, for
four hands, lack opus numbers and remain unpublished. In
September 1880 Chausson composed a Sonata in F minor,
also unnumbered and unpublished. Then came eleven four-
voiced fugues on themes by Bach, Hasse, Franck, Massenet,
and Saint-Saëns, written from October 23, 1880, to August
14, 1881. Still other works were the *Cinq Fantaisies,* Op. 1,
of 1879, and the *Marche militaire* of 1884. Chausson destroyed
the Op. 1 plates after publication in 1880, while *Marche
militaire* remains in manuscript. All of these early works
reveal Chausson in the role of a student: the manuscript of
the F minor sonata shows Massenet's corrections, while the
fugues were intended as disciplinary preparations for the
Prix de Rome. Chausson did submit the fugue on Saint-
Saëns's theme, and *L'Arabe* (also unpublished) for male
chorus, tenor solo, and orchestra in fulfillment of the Prix
de Rome requirements, but the 1881 prize was awarded to
Alfred Bruneau. Chausson's extreme disappointment with
himself was expressed in a letter to Mme de Rayssac.

For the next example of solo piano music, one must proceed to *Quelques danses,* Op. 26, composed in June and July of 1896. This—Chausson's only major work for piano—is composed of four pieces: "Dédicace", "Sarabande", "Pavane", and "Forlane." It was dedicated to Mme Robert de Bonnières, wife of the poet to whom Duparc was indebted for his *mélodie Le Manoir de Rosamonde.* In addition to his poetry, de Bonnières wrote novels and contributed criticisms of writers, both past and present, to various journals; besides Chausson, he counted Anatole France among his friends. Debussy thought very highly of Chausson's little suite and expressed his delight by saying, "one must love them all, these dances"; he singled out the "Sarabande" for special comment.[1]

Although Chausson's career is too short and uneven to be divided into "periods" like those associated with many of the great composers, there is little doubt that in the final two or three years of his life he was tending toward a neoclassical style based on an interest not only in the eighteenth-century French tradition as revealed in the Baroque dances of his suite but also in a more objective and less emotional style than had been his wont. One can see the seeds of the change in *Poème's* balanced structure, although not in its highly charged content. Here, in *Quelques danses*—the very next work after *Poème*—the classical attitude extends to the content as well. This more detached approach is at the heart of French music and demonstrates Chausson's growing independence from the more Germanic emphasis of Franck, and also from the stultifying Wagnerian idiom. Had he lived, this freeing process would undoubtedly have continued.

"Dédicace," in triple meter and marked "calme," is, of course, not one of the formal Baroque dances but a short prelude of one page. Although the key-signature consists of one sharp, there is but one short passage where G major is briefly established. Everything else consists of various types of nonresolving seventh chords as well as ninths, and there is even a trace of whole-tone writing. The right-hand part—it cannot be called a theme or melody—consists entirely of disconnected, syncopated segments. The piece ends on an unresolved dominant seventh chord on D, although the effect is considerably lessened by the use of tied notes. The entire piece does certainly remind one of Debussy's methods, some of which were pointed out in chapter 2 and have been recorded by Maurice Emmanuel from the fascinating conversations between Debussy and his former harmony professor, Ernest Guiraud. One further point from these conversations that has relevance here is Debussy's use of the verb *noyer,* "to drown," with reference to tonality. Emmanuel, in his harmonic analysis of *Pelléas et Mélisande,* lists nine ways by which Debussy accomplished this "drowning" or blurring of tonality, in each case supporting his conclusion with examples from *Pelléas.* However, Emmanuel later makes the very important observation that "never did Debussy push the 'drowning' of the tonality to the point of asphyxiation." [2] This applies to Chausson's "Dédicace," where G major is at least momentarily established. However, one can easily see from this piece how far Chausson had digressed from Franck's fundamental principle that "your tonality must never be in doubt."

"Sarabande," by contrast, is very tonally oriented: B-flat, G minor. Again, a comparison with Debussy is very much in order by virtue of the fact that the second piece of the latter's *Pour le piano* (1896–1901) bears the same title. Although Debussy originally wrote the sarabande in 1894, at which time it formed one of the four *Images* for piano, it was later slightly revised and incorporated in *Pour le piano.*

The traditional framework of triple meter and slow tempo, together with the sarabande's characteristic second-beat accentuation, is present in both dances. However, when we inspect and listen more closely, the differences between Chausson's and Debussy's writing become obvious. Chausson's theme, with certain exceptions, is concentrated in the topmost part and is undergirded with supporting chords of various kinds—the vast majority of them being functional with reference to each other and the tonalities to which they belong. In Debussy's "Sarabande," the attention from the beginning is focused on blocklike parallel chords, to the extent that the listener identifies these as the main theme in addition to the melody in the topmost line that results from the chordal movement. More important, these chords are independent of one another and do not function as members of keys where conventional preparations and resolutions are expected. Chausson employs parallel chords too, but because they are confined to the right-hand part and occur only in the middle of his piece, they seem incidental rather than basically thematic; they are also functional. Confining them to the right hand removes another similarity to Debussy, for the deep sonorities often present in the latter's two-handed parallel writing are lacking. From time to time in Chausson's "Sarabande" there are modal touches that emphasize the "antique" feeling. And, as in Debussy's "Sarabande," no particular era or composer is invoked—least of all the Baroque. Yet the classical detachment that recalls some vague, past era is decidedly present in both sarabandes.

"Pavane," the third piece of *Quelques danses,* is infused with a gentle gravity, urged along by an almost continuous eighth-note movement whose exquisitely graceful flow accentuates the charm of this old dance form. The occasional modality also heightens the expressiveness.

The concluding piece, "Forlane"—an evocation of the *forlana,* a spirited north-Italian dance in $\frac{6}{4}$ meter—is in the nature of a toccata; pianistically, it is difficult. Marked *animé,* its driving rhythm, couched in relentless eighth notes that never cease, is sometimes sharply syncopated. Except for the quieter and less tense middle section, the hands duplicate each other—sometimes one, sometimes two octaves apart. Such parallelism is, of course, a Debussy trait, examples occurring in "Prélude" and "Sarabande" from *Pour le piano*. However, there are subtle differences, for Chausson's parallel construction emphasizes linear movement that results from the rapid tempo of the eighth notes. Debussy, on the other hand, with his slower tempi in both pieces exploits full vertical sonorities.

Quelques danses was first performed on April 3, 1897, by Edouard Risler at the Société Nationale—the same concert at which Thérèse Roger first presented *Serres chaudes* with Risler as accompanist. The latter, then only twenty-four years old, had not yet acquired his great reputation for a soft, delicate touch in which every possible nuance was explored. In addition to the Chausson work, Risler had given first performances of numerous works by Fauré, Dukas, and Samazeuilh.

In retrospect, *Quelques danses,* besides being a charming and well-written set of dances, is important for another reason: it is one of the first piano works to consciously explore the French musical past in a modern synthesis. Although Debussy's *Pour le piano* and Ravel's *Le Tombeau de Couperin* are also important examples of this trend, Chausson's suite is perhaps more significant in his total oeuvre than are the two other composers' works because *Quelques danses* demonstrates a definite departure from the mostly German seriousness of Franck—a problem neither of the others had to face—toward the more detached and objective style one associates with the main line of French music. It is further proof that Chausson's true position is that of a connecting link between Franck and Debussy. Had he lived, it is fair to assume that Chausson would have become even more truly "French" in his outlook and in his music.

Chausson's only remaining piano piece is the short *Paysage,* Op. 38, written in 1895 during one of his Italian sojourns at Fiesole and dedicated to his niece, Mlle Christine Lerolle, the daughter of his artist brother-in-law, Henri Lerolle. The quietly flowing eighth-note movement in the *calme sans lenteur* tempo is broken just once in its four-page length. Dynamic markings are very infrequent and their range is from *mezzo piano* to *piano* only; all but one indication is confined to the first page, the exception being a slight swell at the bottom of the second page.

Except for a short passage in the middle, where there is a limited application of whole-tone writing, simple triads, passing tones, and various kinds of seventh chords, some of which move chromatically, are the norm. The objective, impersonal spirit of *Quelques danses* is missing here, a fact not too surprising when one realizes that *Paysage* was composed a year earlier than the suite despite *Paysage's* later opus number. Thus the opus numbers are not completely reliable indicators of when Chausson's essentially classical style began. The prevailing mood of *Paysage* is one of gentle melancholy, termed by Calvocoressi "discreet and almost unobtrusive . . . (Corot could not paint a more gently sad gray)."[3] Indeed, gray is the appropriate word to use in describing this highly effective little piece.

Chausson's one work for organ, *Les Vêpres du commun des vierges,* Op. 31, dates from the time of the family vacation at the Villa Papiniano in Fiesole, where it was completed on December 15, 1897. A pictorial record of this time is preserved in the painting that Maurice Denis executed of Mme Chausson and her infant son, Laurent, born the preceding year.[4] It was a generally happy and relaxed time for the composer, enlivened by visits from friends among whom were, besides Denis, the Nabi painter Vuillard. *Les Vêpres* originated from a request by the organist and choirmaster of Saint-Gervais, Charles Bordes—one of the Franckists—whose scholarly interest in the music of Josquin des Prez, Lassus, Victoria, and Palestrina, as well as in Gregorian chant, led to the founding of *Les Chanteurs de Saint-Gervais* and, later, with d'Indy, of the Schola Cantorum. Whether Chausson's use of portions of Gregorian chant in this work was inspired by his friendship with Bordes or was a result of prior interest in this field is not clear. *Vêpres,* dedicated to the composer's daughter Annie, received its first performance by the great French organist Charles Tournemire in the hall of the Schola Cantorum on March 2, 1901.

Vêpres consists of eight pieces based on the Gregorian chants for the Common of Virgins at First and Second Vespers, and three others entitled "Autres Antiennes Brêves pour le magnificat." The first eight fall into the following divisions: one through five are based on the corresponding five antiphons prescribed for both First and Second Vespers (*Liber Usualis,* pp. 1210–11). Chausson identifies each by its Latin title and the number of the Gregorian mode. The sixth and eighth pieces are each founded on antiphons for the Magnificat at First and Second Vespers respectively; the text for each is the same ("Veni sponsa Christi") but the chants and modes are different (*Liber Usualis,* p. 1209, 8th mode; p. 1214, 7th mode). The seventh piece is based on the antiphon from Second Vespers, "Prudentes Virgines," to be used "for two or more Virgins, at First and Second Vespers, at the Magnificat" (*Liber Usualis,* p. 1215).

The first five pieces have in common the fact that they are extraordinarily short, ranging from the seven measures of no. 4, "Veni electa mea" to seventeen for no. 5, "Ista est speciosa." On the other hand, nos. 6 through 8 are of normal length: two, five, and four pages respectively. This question of the length of the various pieces is not so unimportant as it might seem, for the durations are remarkably close—as are Chausson's musical treatments of the pieces—to the requirements for a contest involving Gregorian-based organ music, sponsored by the Schola Cantorum and announced in *La Tribune de Saint-Gervais,* the institution's official journal:

> During the month of November there will be a competition for some organ versets in the form of contra-antiphons for the Vespers of St. Mary the Virgin. That is to say, five versets for the five first antiphons plus two more developed

pieces to serve as contra-antiphons for the Magnificat at first and second Vespers. These versets should draw their melodic inspiration from each of the corresponding plain-song antiphons, be conceived in the tonalities of each of them, and not exceed twenty-five to thirty measures in a moderate tempo. Only the two contra-antiphons for the Magnificat may be more developed. . . . We also recommend that the competitors get the antiphons thoroughly in their minds in order to reproduce their feeling as well as the spirit of the end of the psalm.[5]

If one substitutes for the "Vespers of St. Mary the Virgin" the "Vespers of Virgins," he finds that Chausson met the requirements with respect to length. The article from which the above passage was taken continues by saying: "furthermore, by restricting the length of the contra-antiphon the Schola was doubtless trying to make its duration correspond to that of an average antiphon sung according to Dom Pothier's rhythmic interpretation."[6]

Chausson's musical treatment of the individual pieces in *Vêpres* also conforms to the Schola's principles. In every case except the fifth and eighth pieces, free use is made of the opening motive—generally five to eight notes—of the corresponding antiphon. While Chausson does not reproduce every note of these head motives, the melodic contour for at least the first measure or two bears a relationship, though not a perfect resemblance, to the chant. In the fifth and eighth settings the composer is concerned not with the beginning but with the ending of the original chant. This treatment is much more apparent in the eighth piece—one of the Magnificat antiphons—where the length (sixty-one measures) allows for a variety of presentation of the material; some of the appearances are imitative.

Rhythmically, there is considerable freedom, as in the eighth setting where there is a section containing a measure-by-measure alternation of $\frac{2}{2}$ and $\frac{3}{2}$ meter, strongly suggestive of the duple and triple groupings of Gregorian chant. The first piece, "Haec est virgo sapiens et una," is in $\frac{5}{4}$

meter while the sixth, "Veni sponsa Christi," is in $\frac{7}{8}$. In each instance a supple and free-flowing movement results that is more apparent in the longer no. 6, where occasional cross-rhythms are seen. Harmonically, Chausson underlines his melodic lines with chords chosen from the appropriate modes, and takes pains to preserve modal cadences. Sometimes a seventh chord occurs, and chromatic passing and auxiliary tones are found, but these do not disturb the modality for they are merely decorative adjuncts to it.

Chausson's treatment is also flexible with respect to the purpose for which the work was intended. That it was composed to fulfill a liturgical need is clearly indicated by the composer's instructions, printed at the bottoms of appropriate pages. The first such instruction concerns the sixth piece—the first Magnificat antiphon—and tells us on the bottom of page 3 that "if there is no burning of incense, one may pass to the * on page 4"; at the end of the sixth measure on page 3, an asterisk is provided for this purpose. It is confusing, however, to be met on page 4 by *two* asterisks—one near the top, the other near the bottom. At the bottom of this page, one reads, "If one wishes to shorten these antiphons, the organist will find the necessary cadence at the * placed in the course of them." It appears that from measure 6, page 3, the organist may go to the end of either measure 9 or measure 21, page 4, if the service requires the shortened form. In either case, the final chord of the piece may follow these measures as an appropriate cadence. In the seventh setting we are told that "for the office, one may pass to the second *," a cut of thirty-two measures. A similar cut of twenty measures is provided in the eighth piece.

The first two of the three "Autres Antiennes Brêves pour le magnificat"—the remaining pieces of the work—are alternate settings of no. 7, "Prudentes virgines." Although each of them is somewhat shorter than the cut version of no. 7, the main reason for providing them may be a practical one, for the original version even in abbreviated form presents technical difficulties not contained in the much simpler alternates. The third setting is an exact duplicate of the final fifteen measures of no. 8; again, this section is somewhat simpler than the earlier portions of no. 8, and its inclusion in a service context would considerably shorten even the cut version. One wonders, however, why Chausson did not compose a wholly new short version, as he did in the case of "Prudentes virgines."

Thus, with the cuts and the alternate versions, there are made available attractive options. The more advanced organists may use the originals with or without cuts, while the less technically proficient will undoubtedly choose the alternates. These pieces are also thoroughly suitable as recital material—at least the longer ones. Chausson nowhere includes suggestions for registration or manuals to be used; thus the performer is free to exercise his imagination and to change manuals and mix tonal colors at will.

And so here again, in a second major keyboard work, Chausson demonstrated his progressive outlook by composing in line with an important trend that was new, yet looked backward to the great musical past for inspiration. And again, in contradiction to those who see only Franck and Wagner influences at work in his music, he demonstrated his independence, for he could not possibly have derived the modal style of *Vêpres* from any of Franck's organ music, for the very simple reason that the latter contains no modality; Franck's sense of tonality was, as we have seen, too strong and too dominating, and it left no room for modal flavorings. Even "the only organ pieces Franck is known to have written specifically for liturgical use—a posthumously published collection of versets for the Magnificat—are based on original themes, folktunes, and noëls, but not on plainsong."[7] And, according to d'Indy, Franck "knew nothing about the erudite and definitive researches of the Benedictines into the subject of Gregorian music."[8] Thus, along with d'Indy, whose *Vêpres d'un martyr* appeared in 1899, and Alexandre Guilmant, who composed many such Gregorian-based works, Chausson was in the vanguard of a restorative movement that reached a culmination in such nonliturgical works as Charles Marie Widor's *Symphonie gothique* and *Symphonie romane,* and Marcel Dupré's *Vêpres du commun.* All three of these are staples in the recital organist's repertory.

NOTES

1. Quoted in Vallas, *The Theories of Claude Debussy,* p. 47.

2. Emmanuel, *Pelléas et Mélisande de Claude Debussy,* p. 217.

3. Quoted in Barricelli and Weinstein, *Ernest Chausson,* p. 74.

4. This painting is reproduced in Oulmont, *Musique de l'amour,* p. 144.

5. *La Tribune de Saint-Gervais* 3, no. 11 (November 1897): 174–75. Printed in Benjamin Van Wye, "Gregorian Influences in French Organ Music before the *Motu proprio,*" JAMS, 27, no. 1 (Spring 1974):14.

6. Ibid. Dom Pothier was one of the leaders in the Gregorian chant restoration being conducted by the Benedictines at Solesmes.

7. Ibid., p. 7.

8. d'Indy, *César Franck,* p. 130.

5

Music for the Theater

BEGINNING with his student days in 1879 and con-
tinuing until his untimely death twenty years later,
Chausson's enthusiasm for lyric drama, including incidental
music for various plays, remained strong and undiminished.
From the year 1879-80 there are two unpublished fragments—
Jeanne d'Arc and *Esméralda*. The first, to words whose origin
is not known, was apparently intended to be a short scene,
and was scored for soloists, women's chorus, and orchestra. It
was presented January 31, 1881, at the Paris Conservatoire,
where its reception was generally unfavorable—not at all
surprising considering Chausson's apprentice status. The
second fragment, based on Act 4, Scene 1 of Victor Hugo's
drama, consists of Esméralda's aria, of which there are two
versions, one dated April 2, the other December 4, 1880.
At the other end of the spectrum there is Chausson's completed libretto (but no music) of 1899 for his new opera, *La
Vie est un songe*, adapted from a drama by the Spanish play-
wright Calderón.

Between these two extremes there is, not only the completed opera *Le Roi Arthus*—to be considered in some detail
presently—but also two other dramatic works worthy of our
attention. These are *La Tempête*, Op. 18, consisting of incidental music for Shakespeare's comedy; and *La Légende de
Sainte Cécile*, Op. 22, written for Maurice Bouchor's drama
of the same title. In addition, three other minor works should
be mentioned: the unpublished short orchestral entracte
("La Mort de Coelio") for Alfred de Musset's comedy *Les*

Caprices de Marianne, Op. 4—performed five times from 1885 to 1898; *Hélène*, Op. 7, lyric drama in two acts after Leconte de Lisle, from which only a women's chorus has been published; and some interludes for flute and harp (also unpublished) for Aristophanes' *The Birds*. The published excerpt from *Hélène* need not detain us for, although it is competently written, it has no distinguishing features of any kind; melodically, harmonically, and rhythmically it is entirely conventional and predictable.

The incidental music for Aristophanes' *Les Oiseaux*, as well as that for *La Tempête* and *La Légende de Sainte Cécile*, was composed for the performances of these dramas at Le Petit Théâtre de la Galerie Vivienne, a small marionette theater founded in 1888 by the poet Henri Signoret; it was a very successful venture that lasted until 1892. Chausson's friend, Maurice Bouchor, played a very important part in this enterprise from the start for, besides translating *The Tempest* into French and writing his *Légende*, he also wrote for puppets the play *Tobie*, a biblical legend in verse in five tableaux; *Noël, ou le mystère de la nativité*; and the *Mystères d'Éleusis*.

Although the use of puppets rather than live actors, together with the minute size of the theater, necessarily affected the size of the clientele, one should not underestimate the importance of this experiment for, in its small way, it was an avant-garde reaction to the stifling situation in the late nineteenth-century French theater. Like anything that has become too long entrenched through repetition of successful formulae, the theater had ossified to the point where young and talented dramatists found themselves unable to secure a hearing and, in self-defense, had turned to various manifestations of the avant-garde, of which the puppet theater was but one expression.

No less a person than Anatole France wrote enthusiastically of Le Petit Théâtre. In *La Vie littéraire*, volume 2, two essays are devoted to the subject;[1] while in volume 3 there

are two more, one of which is about Bouchor's *Tobie*.[2]
France was utterly captivated by marionettes, and believed
them superior to human actors. "For me," he said, "I feel
a kind of reverence mixed with a sort of tenderness for the
little entities of wood and cardboard, clothed in wool or
satin, that pass before my eyes. . . ."[3] And again, "in the
meantime, I have twice seen the marionettes of the Rue
Vivienne, and I have taken great pleasure in them. I have an
infinite desire to replace living actors with them. If I must
speak further, actors spoil the play for me. . . their talent
is too great: it covers everything . . . their person effaces the
work they are performing."[4] Paul Margueritte, one of the
avant-gardists, introduced the Petit Théâtre to the public by
means of a brochure. His remarks in support of marionettes
in this booklet were quoted by France and, in effect, say the
same thing: marionettes are superior to human actors by
virtue of their impersonality. Yet, "in their essential gestures
is held the complete expression of human feelings."[5] Unfortunately, nowhere in his essays did France mention any
of the incidental music for these little dramas.

As for puppet manipulation, an advanced technique was
developed at Le Petit Théâtre, where "the puppets had a
remarkable method of control, being mounted on rods fixed
in a base moving on rails below stage, movements of limbs
by strings attached to pedals; dialogue was spoken by separate
group(s) of performers."[6]

The music for Chausson's *La Tempête*, the first of his
musical settings for marionettes, was scored for a violin,
flute, harp, celesta, and voices. It consists of five sections as
follows: "Chant d'Ariel," "Air de danse," "Duo de Junon
et Cérès," "Danse rustique," and "Chanson d'Ariel." Each
of these sections corresponds to the appropriate place in
Shakespeare's drama, and each number catches the mood of
the scene for which it was written. There is a charm and fresh-
ness that pervade the entire score, but, as usual, there were
critics who saw nothing there at all. Dedicated to Henri

Signoret, founder of the marionette theater, the music was first performed in December 1888 with Anatole France, the poets Théodore de Banville and Jean Richepin, the eminent philosopher and historian Ernest Renan, and the critic and dramatist Jules Lemaître in attendance.

A far more important and significant work—especially in Bouchor's oeuvre—is *La Légende de Sainte Cécile*, Op. 22. Scored for soloists, women's chorus, and small orchestra, it was begun in the summer of 1891 and finished on the following September 28. Chausson dedicated it to his friend Raymond Bonheur, friend of Debussy, composer, and dedicatee of the latter's *Prélude à l'aprés-midi d'un faune.*

Bouchor's drama was next to the last in his series of religious plays for marionettes. Both Le Petit Théâtre and the shadow theater of the famous Montmartre cabaret, Le Chat Noir, played a large part in the mystical revival that swept over Paris in the early 1890s. When viewed in the light of the criticism in *Art et Critique*, 2 (1890) that "the only theatre doing anything artistic just has to be a theatre of marionettes,"[7] one cannot but question the remark of Barricelli and Weinstein concerning the *Légende*: "certainly no one could have mistaken it for a serious religious drama, especially when it was written for Le Petit Théâtre des Marionettes!"[8] It was, in fact, such a serious drama that "some critics found it too much for puppets to convey."[9] With respect to its plot,

> Bouchor reproduces some of the popular elements of his earlier Mystery plays, with a conflict between the simple, pious character and the vulgar, gluttonous heathen, and with the same introductory apology, which with mock preciosity takes the audience into the author's confidence over such details as puppet strings and similar embarrassments [a short confidential introduction, minus the puppet details, also opens *La Tempête*]. This direct, fresh approach establishes the indispensable link between the audience and players. . . . Cécile, the young Christian, converts

her non-Christian lover, Valérien, and the two prepare to die together as an act of faith at the hands of Gaymas, who is the typical king's henchman of the medieval play in which farce and piety are combined. The chaste lovers die, in spite of the pagan king's having been carried off to hell. . . . Cécile is beatified against a background of heavenly choirs.[10]

The *Légende* is composed of three acts, with a further division into fifteen tableaux—six in the first and third acts, and three in the second. Chausson's music for these scenes is very uneven in quality, reaching its finest point in the seventh tableau (Scene 1 of Act 2), "Cantique de Cécile"; here a short cello solo precedes Cécile's simple and moving prayer to the Virgin. Some of the purely orchestral tableaux are also effective, particularly nos. 3, 4 and 5. In no. 3 St. Michael, with sword in hand, encourages and champions the doomed lovers. With their triple meter, modal flavor, and martial atmosphere, these three tableaux strongly recall the famed medieval Agincourt Song. No. 5 is an exact duplicate of most of no. 4 until a meter and tempo change signals the entrance of Valérien, at which point a reminiscence of the opening theme of no. 2 is heard. No. 3, "Hymne liturgique de St. Michel" is an extremely abbreviated setting in unison of the first part of the two following scenes. Several of the tableaux, including nos. 4 and 5, are called "Mélodrame," while others are entitled "Musique de scène."

Chausson's music for the choir of angels (Act 1, Scenes 2, 6; Act 3, all tableaux except no. 14) is the weakest part of his score. Set for a women's chorus of first and second soprano, and contralto, most of the writing is in block form. In the majority of instances, the harmonies are so usual as to be banal. When the angels are justifiably indignant at the blasphemy of the pagan king—an act that leads to his untimely demise—the harmony is excitedly chromatic, accompanied by storming figures, loud chords, and seething tremolos in the orchestra. During the more tranquil passages, arpeggiated string and harp figures abound, although even here the chromaticism can be rather startling at times. And very surprisingly, the text accentuation is mediocre, even poor in places, leading one to think that the words were made to conform to the music. And yet all of the clichés just enumerated probably sound no worse than those found in some of the Gounod Masses, as well as in Franck's Mass in A major and *Les Béatitudes*. This era was not, after all, one of the great moments in French choral music, for most of the works in this category were feeble, cliché-ridden, slightly saccharine, and entirely lacking in imagination. Even Debussy's *La Damoiselle élue* rises only slightly above this standard. In Chausson's case, however, his choral writing had vastly improved by 1897 in "Chant funèbre," and it can be said that the improvement was a matter of evolution and deeper experience, whereas in the choral music of Gounod and Franck a certain smug adherence to successful formulae can be sensed.

That Chausson's only completed opera, *Le Roi Arthus*, Op. 23, which occupied its composer from 1886 to 1895, was never intended to stand alone as the only "drame lyrique" in his oeuvre, is amply proved by the accompanying list of projected dramatic works, found recently in a little black noteboook:[11]

I.   *Les Bohémiens*, d'après Pouchkine. Drame lyrique en deux actes (mai 1882).

II.   *Tourandocte*, comédie lyrique en trois actes, imitée de Schiller.

III.   *Macbeth*, drame lyrique en trois actes, d'après Shakespeare.

IV.   *Conrad Wallenrood*, poème dramatique en trois actes, d'après Mickiewicz.

V.   *Le Roi Arthus*, drame lyrique en trois actes.

VI.   *Rama*, drame lyrique en trois actes.

VII.   *Numance*, drame lyrique en trois actes et quatre tableaux, d'après Cervantes (Henry Barraud).

Considering the amount of time Chausson lavished on *Le Roi Arthus* and the central position it occupied in his life, the statement that "the composer himself regarded [it] as only an experiment"[12] seems extreme and untenable, particularly in view of the efforts made by the composer to get the opera produced in Kassel, Dresden, and Prague—efforts that met with dismal failure. It finally received its first performance November 30, 1903 at Brussel's Théâtre de la Monnaie with Mme Chausson, Henri Lerolle (who assisted with the set designs), Odilon Redon, d'Indy, Fauré, various Parisian critics, and other notables, including royalty, in attendance.

It is unfortunate that many French operas written during and immediately after Wagner's lifetime must be considered in relation to "old Klingsor, alias R. Wagner," as Debussy called him.[13] Even such a rebelliously anti-Wagnerian opera as *Pelléas et Mélisande* has its moments; and when Chausson dolefully refers to *Arthus* as "Wagnerian in subject and Wagnerian in music," and asks, "is that not too much altogether?",[14] the obligation to undertake a study of his opera in terms of a close comparison with Wagner is obvious, if for no other reason than to assess the accuracy of the composer's judgment as well as that of others. Thus *Arthus* finds itself in the same position as the Symphony in B-flat major except that, in the case of the opera, there are two diametrically opposed points of view. One of these extremes is held by Martin Cooper, when he says that Chausson's "darling work which caused him so much heart-burning, the opera *Le Roi Arthus*, is, alas! impeccably Wagnerian from beginning to end."[15] At the other end of the critical spectrum, Barricelli and Weinstein assert that "any comparison between the two composers which means to go beyond the external analogy of the same legendary cycle is both useless and dangerous."[16] Apparently these defenders overlooked Chausson's own assessment (or refused to believe it), quoted above from their own book. As usual, the truth lies somewhere between the two extremes.

First and foremost among the Wagnerian influences on *Le Roi Arthus* are the external parallels in subject matter between this work and *Tristan und Isolde*. There is the illicit love affair between Lancelot and Guinevere, carried on behind Arthur's back; Lionel, Lancelot's faithful friend, takes the place of Kurvenal and also doubles as Brangeane, for it is he who warns the lovers of the approaching daybreak; and Melot's treachery is carried out by Mordred. The analogy ends here, for the forces set in motion by the lovers lead, in each instance, to quite different conclusions: Chausson, like Wagner the author of his libretto, chooses to introduce the moral aspects of the problem by emphasizing Lancelot's sense of guilt, while Wagner in *Tristan* glorifies the illicit relationship. Barricelli and Weinstein sum up these differences in the following passage:

> If now we analyze the German's and the Frenchman's character portrayals closely, we are immediately struck by the difference in the behavior of the knights after their sins. In the former's work, where King Mark is relegated to a secondary plane and the interest revolves around the two lovers, we witness the triumph and apotheosis of a fatal and inexorable erotic passion, whereas in the latter's, where Arthur takes the foreground, we are presented with an exaltation of duty, beauty, and moral grandeur. Next to him, Lancelot actually seeks death, after having torn himself away from Guinevere, because he recognizes the guilt of his love and can only hope to justify himself by expiation. This situation brings out the philosophy of the drama. Guinevere, in her criminal passion and Lancelot, in his faithless weakness, are extinguished in a demise without honor.[17]

Chausson's title, chosen it would seem very deliberately, emphasizes the centrality of Arthur and shows us something, moreover, of Chausson's own character through his interest in developing Arthur as the personification of all that is noble and good. And, of course, the illicit love affair emerges as one of the important molders of Arthur's character. Thus the underlying philosophy of each drama is fundamentally different. In his penetrating discussion of *Arthus*,[18] Gallois elaborates on these differences and points out that Chausson's opera is essentially a Christian drama in which spiritual truths and attitudes are predominant. Consequently the opera sheds as much light on Chausson's prevailing philosophy of life as any of his correspondence or recorded utterances. Viewed in this way, the importance of *Arthus* in Chausson's life becomes as vital as all of his correspondence indicates, and the idea of the opera's being "only an experiment" grows even more untenable.

Arthus consists of three acts, each of which is divided into two tableaux. Each act is introduced by an orchestral prelude, a clear reference to the Wagnerian music drama rather than to the conventional opera, where overtures are employed, and there is an orchestral transition between the tableaux in the manner of *Pelléas*. Nowhere in the opera is there any Wagnerian *leitmotiv* system. It is true that a broad and heroic theme symbolizing Arthur occurs several times in the course of the work, as does a theme associated with the love of Lancelot and Guinevere; but neither is ever varied in conformity with changing situations in the manner of Wagner, and they never assume significant places in the orchestral fabric as instigators or barometers of action. They seem, rather, to have been conceived like the curse motive and Sparafucile's music in *Rigoletto*: central, unchangeable themes that recur at strategic moments.

It would be difficult to find anything less Wagnerian than the Prelude to Act 1, a large part of which consists of a galloping, triplet figure whose melodic fragments are announced in various keys in the manner of a quasi-symphonic development; the same is true of the first tableau, whose action takes place in Arthur's court. The King, surrounded by his knights, narrates his victory over the Saxons, expresses his joy and contentment at the return of peace, and publicly praises Lancelot for his valor. Guinevere's aria contains her congratulations. Mordred is furious, and plots vengeance to one side with a group of malcontents, his fury growing as he overhears Guinevere's hurried whisper to Lancelot concerning their approaching nocturnal tryst. The style throughout this first tableau is almost entirely diatonic. What chromaticism there is is used in two ways: as decorations within the boundaries of keys, and as agents of modulation. When it is employed in the second way, the suspensions, appoggiaturas, and voice leadings that together form a large part of Wagner's chromaticism are missing, for Chausson's chromaticism is contained in block chords. An example of the decorative use to which Chausson puts his chromaticism may be seen in the following excerpt from the accompaniment to Guinevere's aria.

Fig. 26. Chausson; *Le Roi Arthus,* 1, p. 37, mm. 2–3

On the third beat of each measure may be seen the flatted sixths so often present in the *mélodies*. A little later in the same aria, chromaticism is used as a modulatory agent (Figure 27).

Fig. 27. Chausson; *Le Roi Arthus,* 1, p. 38, mm. 3–6

Stylistically, this accompaniment belongs to the older operatic tradition, with its stereotyped rhythms, accented basses, and conventional accompaniment figures. The last may be seen, continuously repeated, in the sections preceding Guinevere's aria, where some of the figures are arpeggiated chords while others are triplets. The very fact that we can employ such words as *aria* and *accompaniment* suggests how far from Wagnerian practices we are, to say nothing concerning the type of music Chausson found suitable for this first tableau.

The second tableau contains the love duet, the first and third sections of which conduct us into the world of *Tristan*; the Wagner influence is less obvious in the middle section. Three external similarities to the *Tristan* love duet, noticeable at the very beginning, are the key (A-flat major), the meter ($\frac{3}{4}$), and the A-flat pedal point in the orchestra, which

Chausson holds for four measures as against Wagner's sixteen. The chromaticism in the vocal and orchestral parts
proceeds stepwise; there is some contrary motion in the
vocal parts; and cadences are often postponed or avoided—
all notable features of the *Tristan* duet. The first two of these
just-noted characteristics appear at the start of Chausson's
duet, while a little farther along, the third trait materializes
as a result of appoggiaturas. However, each of these typical
Wagnerian techniques is found less frequently in Chausson's
duet.

Thus far, only similarities between the two love duets
have been noted, yet there are differences in the handling of
technical means that should be mentioned. The first of these
is in the rhythmic area. A study of the first section of Chausson's duet reveals a certain inflexibility in that the pattern
of movement in each voice part is identical, while to a lesser
extent, the vocal patterns are reproduced in the orchestra—
although there are exceptions caused by syncopations in the
accompaniment. Even so, the rhythmic interplay between
voices and between voices and orchestra does not achieve
the level of variety and flexibility that is apparent throughout much of Wagner's duet. Except for the first appearance
of the "Liebestod" at the end of his duet, where the rhythmic
patterns tend to be undeviating, Wagner often changes his
patterns, opposes one to another, and, in some instances,
has three going simultaneously.

Another way in which Wagner introduces variety is by
allowing his vocal lines to imitate one another; at times,
this amounts almost to a canon between the voices. Finally,
there is more variety and flexibility in Wagner's chromatic
harmony, which is not only more pervasive than Chausson's,
but also goes farther afield. Elliott Zuckerman notes its
expansiveness when he observes that "in the love-duet,
for example, there are twenty-two measures (from Tristan's
words 'Tristan du'. . . .) during which the bass moves down
the chromatic scale through two octaves."[19]

Before we move to a consideration of the second act of
Chausson's opera, mention should be made of a striking
resemblance—amounting for all practical purposes to a
quotation—between a passage in the orchestral interlude
preceding Chausson's love duet and one in the Prelude to
Act 2 of *Tristan*. The mood of the Prelude is one of impatience
as Wagner's lovers await their tryst. Chausson's interlude
is a transition between a scene at Arthur's court and the
clandestine meeting of the Queen and Lancelot, and, as such,
contains the boisterous, rapid music of the festive court scene
before a slow section prepares us for the impending duet.
However, Guinevere's final words in the scene about to end
are a reminder to Lancelot of their coming meeting. It therefore seems reasonable that a note of impatience crept into
the interlude, not unlike that expressed in the *Tristan* Act
2 Prelude, as we can see in the following comparison:

Fig. 28. Chausson; *Le Roi Arthus,* 1, p. 44, mm. 2–5
Wagner; *Tristan,* Prelude 2, mm. 39–42

The Prelude to Act 2 is, in its own way, just as unlike Wagner as the Prelude to Act 1. In fact, the very beginning of it has unmistakable reminders of Debussy, brought about by exact parallelisms in the chords of both hands in the piano-vocal score; these represent, of course, identical chords shared in the upper and lower instruments of Chausson's orchestra. The resultant sonority is a Debussy characteristic, as is the trace of pentatonicism also found in the Prelude.

The first tableau of the second act is concerned with the second meeting of Lancelot and Guinevere. In this scene, Lancelot is filled with remorse and guilt over his infidelity to Arthur, while the thoroughly unrepentant Guinevere loudly demands that her lover save her honor. This apparently irreconcilable difference is temporarily overcome, and the scene ends with the two singing an impassioned duet. The music throughout the scene is, of course, descriptive of the overwrought emotional condition of the lovers and, as such, the temptation to borrow from *Tristan*—either consciously or unconsciously—proved to be irresistible. It is not that there are references to specific passages, but rather that Chausson utilizes some of the individual components of Wagner's style and assembles them in the same way as they are found in *Tristan's* most excitable moments. These components are four in number: chromaticism; sequences; nervous, jerky rhythms; and the *Tristan* Chord. The chromaticism is compounded and urged upward toward a climax by the ascending sequences, the nervous rhythms contribute to the tension, and the climax frequently features the *Tristan* Chord. Up to this point sequences have played a relatively minor role in Chausson's music; their abundance here can probably be explained by the presumption that Chausson, like Wagner, was quick to see that, in a dramatic situation, rising sequences generate steadily increasing excitement and tension. The *Tristan* Chord is also much in evidence in this scene; and is highlighted rather often by being prolonged and by having most of its notes executed by a tremolo. Wagner, on the other hand, is more likely to save the tremolo appearances of the Chord for highly dramatic moments such as the climax of the Prelude to Act 1, and the drinking of the love-potion.

In the midst of these Wagnerian reminiscences, there are likely to be passages that could have come from almost any non-Wagner nineteenth-century opera; one appears below as Figure 29. Despite the presence of some chromaticism, such passages are fundamentally diatonic. They emphasize the disparate elements in this opera, and lead one to believe that they may result from an attempt on Chausson's part to be less Wagnerian, for they do not really convince one as having been planned. Wagner, however, introduces his few diatonic passages in *Tristan* as "deliberate departures, 'specters of day' intruding into the all-prevailing night of the

Fig. 29. Chausson; *Le Roi Arthus,* 2, p. 145, mm. 4–9

love drama."[20] Such uses of diatonicism apply particularly to the music of the sailors' choruses in Act 1, where Wagner seems to be emphasizing the noninvolvement of the sailors in the emotional world of Tristan and Isolde. Even Kurvenal's first-act music is diatonic, as if to represent his lack of sympathy and understanding for Isolde's dark mood prior to her complete involvement with Tristan. However, in the third act, his music is chromatic—a symbol of his total identification with and sympathy for the utterly impossible situation in which the lovers find themselves.

The orchestral interlude connecting this scene with the fourth tableau gradually leads us from the world of passion and duplicity to that of Arthur and his court as the King's heroic theme is sounded again. Arthur, filled with doubts, invokes the aid of his old magician Merlin, much as Wotan consulted Erda in his moment of crisis. Merlin's prophecy is filled with gloom: Arthur will soon die, and the Order of the Round Table will be destroyed. As the act closes, the King prepares to make war against his dissident knights.

In order to understand the contradictory elements in *Le Roi Arthus*, it is important to realize that the composition of this opera consumed parts of nine years of Chausson's life. Work was interrupted a number of times, owing either to a temporary loss of interest or a preoccupation with other projects, like the Symphony. Late in 1893, however, Chausson returned to it. By that time, Chausson and Debussy had become close friends and were corresponding regularly. In an undated letter, believed by Barricelli and Weinstein to have been written in October or November 1893, Chausson informed Debussy:

As for myself, I have taken up again, and without too much trouble, my third act. I am not dissatisfied with what I am writing at the moment. It seems to me that it is becoming clear and de-wagnerized. My wife for whom I played the first scene told me that she almost did not recognize me. But I suppose that is a bit exaggerated.

Otherwise, can you imagine me in a position of having to do the first two acts all over again! That would be equivalent to abandoning the drama, because I feel incapable of going over all that again. It is time to finish it and go on to something else.[21]

Chausson's efforts to "de-wagnerize" himself appear to have borne fruit, for the third act of his opera is the least Wagnerian of all. In place of the Wagnerian influence, there are numerous passages that, like those mentioned above in connection with the second act, could have come from almost any non-Wagner opera of the period. There is still chromaticism to be seen, but instead of employing Wagnerian complexities, Chausson resorted to simpler means such as bodily movement of chromatic chords. As for the chords themselves, there is less dependence in this act on the *Tristan* Chord and more emphasis on the old nineteenth-century cliché: the diminished seventh. Many of the chords— regardless of classification—are arpeggiated and broken up into tremolos.

The action of this fifth tableau is brief: the Queen and an attendant are observing the raging battle in the distance between Arthur's loyal knights and those who, under Mordred's command, have deserted him. The King now knows the full horror of Guinevere's and Lancelot's guilt. Presently, Lancelot, disheveled and wounded, approaches the Queen and her attendant. Understanding now the full implications of his acts, he invites the Queen to taste death with him. Leaving her ingloriously to her fate, Lancelot returns to battle to find death with honor. After a short monologue, Guinevere strangles herself with her long hair, a scene that immediately brings to mind Act 3, Scene 1 of *Pelléas et Mélisande*, where Mélisande's long hair cascades down the outer walls as Pelléas waits below. However, as *Le Roi Arthus* is in no way a Symbolist drama, no real analogy is possible. Chausson's granddaughter-in-law told me that the idea for the strangulation death of Guinevere came to the composer one day when he playfully tied the long hair of his godchild around her throat, unwittingly terrifying her.

The final tableau of the opera is primarily taken up with Arthur's apotheosis by the edge of the sea immediately after the old King has spoken briefly with the dying Lancelot. A barge appears to take Arthur away as two invisible choirs and five on-stage soprano soloists promise him rest from his labors and disappointments, and reward for his idealism and vision in establishing the Order of the Round Table. It is the invisible choirs that are of interest to us here, for comparisons between them and Wagner's off-stage choirs in the first and third acts of *Parsifal* are immediately suggested. Upon close examination, however, it is obvious that the treatment is entirely different. In both of his Grail Temple scenes, Wagner provides a symbolic link between earth—represented by the chorus of knights—and the angelic regions by beginning his Grail music in the knights' chorus, and letting it slowly ascend through the ranks of the two invisible choruses. When the link is completed and all choirs are singing together, variety and interest are maintained by a staggering of parts and the juxtaposition of different rhythmic patterns. At one point, the illusion of a direct pathway between earth and heaven is heightened by the dropping out of parts in the lower choirs until, at the end of the passage, only the highest voices in the topmost choir remain. The unity existing between earthly and spiritual forces is dramatized by the fact that all choirs sing the same words, although at different times. Throughout these passages there is, as Grout says, "an impression in music of actual space and depth."[22]

Such an impression is largely missing in Chausson's treatment of his invisible choirs, for in place of Wagner's flexible choral technique with its careful balance and distribution of parts, Chausson substitutes massed choral effects brought about by extended sections in which both choirs sing together. Much of the time all eight parts are represented;

occasionally, the total is increased when parts are divided. However, not all of this massed effect consists of genuine eight-part writing, for there are places where the choirs either duplicate one another, or parts are only slightly dissimilar. The five soprano soloists add weight to the ensemble; their music consists of unison passages, independent parts, and a combination of the latter with parts borrowed from the soprano lines of the choruses.

All of what has just been described is, of course, totally different from Wagner's concept. The differences in musical material are just as great. In the area of rhythm, for example, most of Chausson's entire scene moves in massive blocks that, in one instance, comprise forty-five measures of continuous choral singing, of which only four do not contain the pattern of two dotted quarters. Throughout the scene, all parts in the separate as well as in the combined choirs often show a vertical alignment of the same rhythmic patterns. These characteristics are in complete contrast to Wagner's third-act choruses, in which not only the patterns differ among themselves, but also the staggered entrances, the dropping out of parts, and the frequent use of rests create new patterns of texture.

Harmonically, there are also wide differences between the scenes. Wagner, beginning in the second measure of page 273, employs a portion of his Grail motive (the "Dresden Amen") as modulatory material in moving from D major to B major through the circle of dominants. The harmony in this passage is thus diatonic—the style Wagner consistently employs for his Grail music. The upward-moving harmonic progressions, working together with the disposition of thematic material in the upper voices of the hierarchy of choirs, obviously fulfill Wagner's intent of suggesting a bridge between earth and heaven. Chausson's harmony in some of his choral passages is essentially diatonic, but with a mixture of chromatic elements. In the passage shown in Figure 30—sung by the second choir—it will be noted that there are three diatonic plateaus undergirded by held notes; the parts above

Fig. 30. Chausson; *Le Roi Arthus,* 3, p. 333, m. 3—p. 335, m. 2

are moving in sequential melodic chromaticism. Chausson's block rhythms are prominent in this passage, part of another large section consisting of forty-seven measures; the illustrated quarter-note movement is featured throughout most of it.

Another difference between this extended section and Wagner's choral passages in *Parsifal* is that, with the exception of two measures, Chausson's second choir is wordless—only "ah" being sung. The same is true in the earlier, forty-five measure section, but there both choirs are wordless throughout. In both sections words are sung by other groups, but these do little to dispel the impression that Chausson is primarily interested throughout the entire scene in other-worldly, atmospheric effects. The gently undulating chromatic chords of Figure 30 help to further this view, for they are not organic in the sense of Wagner's harmony, which participates directly in the action.

It is probably impossible to reach any kind of definitive

verdict regarding a work as large and as important as *Le Roi Arthus* by merely studying the score. An opera lives only when it is seen and heard in its totality on stage as a human drama, and not as an assemblage of notes, words, and stage directions. However, it certainly does not appear that a performance of it is likely to occur at any time in the near future, and final judgments must be reserved until that opportunity, no matter how far in the future it may be. Yet, to leave Chausson's opera in its present negative state with respect to how Wagnerian it is or is not is manifestly unfair and unjust; no work of art should have to live or die by such ridiculous standards, especially one that cost its creator so much worry and anguish. The following remarks, therefore, are intended as a kind of "interim report" based on observation and study of the entire score.

I begin with an emphatic disavowal of the irresponsible and completely unfounded statement cited earlier in this chapter, that *Le Roi Arthus* is "impeccably Wagnerian from beginning to end." It is, as I have shown, Wagnerian in those sections only where the story elements are similar to *Tristan* (the love-duet, and so on); but it is very significant that in the whole of the third act, where Chausson's own libretto poses moral dilemmas and attempts solutions based on age-old questions of guilt and accountability, the composer becomes himself. And if, in becoming himself, he fell back on certain stock-in-trade techniques or procedures, so be it! At least he employed the latter in a powerful way, for his third-act text—convincing and powerful as a literary effort—seems to have brought forth his best musical efforts. This observation concerning the superiority of the third act is borne out by the revivals that featured this act only (Paris opera, March, 1916; a radio performance April 25, 1934). Laurence Davies, in his recent work *César Franck and His Circle*, also stresses the excellence of Act 3.[23] The entire opera was revived, apparently in concert form, June 24, 1949, in commemoration of the fiftieth anniversary of the year of Chausson's death.

And to demonstrate that the public is not entirely lacking in discrimination, the Brussels paper, *Théatra*, conducted a poll in 1909 of opera enthusiasts to determine which operas they would like to see performed at the Théâtre de la Monnaie that season, and obtained the following interesting result: *Le Roi Arthus* was in fourth place with 1,199 votes. *Tristan*, *Pelléas*, and *Götterdämmerung* led the poll, while such operas as *La Bohème* and *Madama Butterfly* brought up the rear; even Mozart's *Die Zauberflöte* and *Don Giovanni* trailed the Chausson opera.

Most of the critics were, for once, on Chausson's side after the first performance; but unfortunately he was not alive to enjoy his success. Such phrases as *very strong, high degree of inspiration, exceptional power of expression*, and a *lyrical temperament infinitely moving and comprehensive*[24] were to be found in the press. Words like these are not tossed around carelessly and indiscriminately by reviewers who covet reputations for competence and accuracy, and their enthusiastic praise makes one all the more eager to someday hear and see *Le Roi Arthus* for himself.

NOTES

1. France, *La Vie littéraire*, "Les Marionnettes de M. Signoret," 2:145-50; and "La Tempete," 2:292-300.

2. France, *La Vie littéraire*, "Hrotswitha aux Marionnettes," 3:10-19; and "M. Maurice Bouchor," 3:218-28.

3. "La Tempête," pp. 292-93.

4. "Les Marionnettes de M. Signoret," p. 148.

5. "La Tempête," p. 293.

6. A. R. Philpott, *Dictonary of Puppetry* (Boston: Plays, Inc., 1969), p. 184, entry for *Le Petit Théâtre*.

7. John A. Henderson, *The First Avant-Garde* (1887-1894) (London: George G. Harrap & Co., Ltd., 1971), p. 124.

8. Barricelli and Weinstein, *Ernest Chausson*, pp. 184-85.

9. Henderson, *The First Avant-Garde*, p. 125.

10. Ibid.

11. Reproduced in Feschotte, "Chausson et la poésie," 4.

12. Grout, *A Short History of Opera*, p. 420.

13. Letter of Monday, October 2, 1893 to Chausson.

14. Letter of 1886 to Paul Poujaud. Previously cited in n. 112, chap. 1.

15. Cooper, *French Music,* p. 66.

16. Barricelli and Weinstein, *Ernest Chausson,* p. 192.

17. Ibid., p. 196. The complete account of the story elements of *Le Roi Arthus* appears on pp. 187-90.

18. Gallois, *Ernest Chausson,* pp. 114-29.

19. Zuckerman, *The First Hundred Years of Wagner's Tristan,* p. 19.

20. Grout, *A Short History of Opera,* p. 397.

21. Barricelli and Weinstein, *Ernest Chausson*, p. 67n. The quotation from the letter is contained on the same page.

22. Grout, *A Short History of Opera,* p. 405.

23. Davies, *César Franck and His Circle*, p. 198.

24. Quoted in Gallois, *Ernest Chausson,* p. 130.

6

Chamber Music

ALTHOUGH Chausson's total contribution to the chamber music repertory is very limited—five works in all, the quality is very substantial. As in the area of dramatic music, his interest was kindled early and maintained itself throughout his life. In fact, it can literally be said that chamber music occupied him right up to his death, for it was the String Quartet in C minor, Op. 35, that he was composing that fateful day in June 1899.

Chausson's first chamber work, Trio in G minor for piano, violin, and cello, Op. 3, was composed in the summer and fall of 1881, and given its first hearing at the Société Nationale April 8, 1882, with the composer André Messager at the piano. Since Chausson was studying composition at the time with Franck, it is practically a foregone conclusion that the Trio will contain influences of one kind or another; the most important of these is in the area of cyclical form. Since Franck's celebrated Quintet was first performed in 1880, and is a very thoroughgoing model of cyclical procedures, it loomed large on Chausson's horizon in terms of structure. Examples of this typically Franckian characteristic in the Trio occur as early as the third movement—marked *assez lent*—where the principal theme is a slow variant of the first movement's second theme. Expressively, this slow movement is an early example of the elegiac style associated with so many of Chausson's works. In the fourth movement all four themes from the first movement are reviewed in somewhat altered form. The second movement, *vite* and in $\frac{3}{8}$ meter, has a lively wit and charm not unlike Mendelssohn.

The first chamber work of Chausson's maturity—Concert in D major for piano, solo violin, and string quartet—occupied the composer from 1889 to July 8, 1891. Its four movements were not written in succession nor were they completed in the same place, an exception to the latter being the first and fourth movements: Civray, June 25 and July 8, 1891. The third movement dates from May 1889 at Crémault, while the second movement was finished in 1890 at Ayssac. This one work alone thus gives us a fascinating picture of the restless comings and goings of a composer for whom a frequent change of scene was an absolute necessity. The Concert presented problems for Chausson, as can be seen from a letter of 1891, written in Civray, in which he speaks of the work as "another failure."[1] Apparently Franck, to whom he showed it in its unfinished state in late August or early September of 1890, had reservations, for Chausson reported that "it pleased him less" than the Symphony in B-flat, which Franck had also seen during the same visit.[2]

Chausson employed the term *Concert* rather than *Concerto* as the title for his new work in an apparent effort to define, perhaps negatively, the role of the solo instruments, for they are *not* to be thought of as solo instruments in the double-concerto sense, but rather as projections against the string quartet background. This is substantially the meaning in Barricelli's and Weinstein's footnote where the term is clarified, although they use the word *blend* to describe the effect of the solo instruments with relation to the string quartet—a word that seems inaccurate in some ways because both the piano and solo violin have dominating roles.[3] Gallois poses the problem somewhat differently by inquiring as to whether the Concert is an attempt to return to the style of the Baroque concerto grosso, with its contrast of two soloists against a small orchestral background.[4] If Chausson did intend the work in this last sense, then it is a failure just as surely as if it is interpreted in the modern, double-concerto context. A string quartet is simply too light and unconvincing a background—even bland is not too harsh a word—to function as support for a solo piano and violin in *any* kind of concerto capacity, Baroque or modern. For one thing, there is no formal organization into anything remotely resembling Baroque *ritornelli*, because the material is not Baroque, but late Romantic in its conception and expression. In fact, the more one becomes familiar with the work through study and repeated hearings, the more convinced one becomes that he is listening to one of the most intense and passionate outpourings in all nineteenth-century chamber music. The lightness of the string quartet background is disappointing only so long as the usual connotations of the word *concerto* are kept in mind; this is particularly so if one tries to force the work into the double-concerto mold. If, however, one thinks of it as a chamber work of unusual design, a sextet perhaps, in which the solo violin and piano often function in the manner of a violin and piano sonata against the quartet, with the latter taking a very active part in the proceedings, the work falls into proper perspective. In any event, this unusual combination has produced results that are bold, immensely effective, and emotionally satisfying. It is a difficult work, requiring virtuoso performances from both soloists.

The Concert is, like the Trio, a cyclical work, but on a far less obvious plane. The first movement, marked *décidé*, opens with a slow, brooding, thirty-four measure introduction dominated by a three-note, motto-like motive (Figure 31) that is shared by all instruments; it is presented at various pitch levels and with different intervallic relationships. With the arrival of measure 35, a sonata-allegro movement (*animé*) unfolds in which the three-note cell forms the head of the first theme. The latter, heard first in the solo violin, is a two-part affair, with the second part excitedly growing out of the first half. The lyrical second theme is presented first in embryonic form by the solo instruments

Fig. 31. Chausson; Concert, 1, mm. 1–2

before its full, complete appearance; this is a favorite technique of the Franckists, and was used in *Poème*. Its full statement in the solo violin is what Barricelli and Weinstein mistakenly call the third theme, their second being the latter half of the first. The development section (and here I employ the term in the sense of Romantic development, where the working-out process is restricted to more or less complete statements of themes in various keys) commences with statements by viola and cello of the three-note figure. This motive also rather insistently separates the development into two parts, with Theme 1 receiving treatment in the first half, and Theme 2 in the second. The motive is also effectively present throughout the second part as a restless undertone to the second theme; thus a more organic developmental technique is introduced. After the recapitulation, the movement ends in a very quiet coda with a final reiteration of the motto. The latter, brooding and sometimes menacing, has served as a reference point throughout the movement in a most aesthetically satisfying way, for it has provided unity and yet has contrasted well with the principal themes.

The second movement is a short, graceful *sicilienne* in ternary form, a very satisfying and calm transition between the rhapsodic, passionate first movement and the intensely tragic third. The latter, marked *grave*, is a tremendous out-pouring of despair and pessimism, one of the really remarkable slow movements in all chamber music. It is a large ternary form, unified by a restless, rocking chromatic figure that is present throughout most of the movement; it begins in the piano where it undergirds the elegiac theme announced by the solo violin. The piano reinforces the violin theme in the right-hand part, emphasizing it at important points with rolled chords, while the chromatic figure moves rest-lessly on in the left hand. In the second section of the ternary form, the piano's chromaticism becomes menacing under a wildly desolate theme assigned to the solo violin. A quiet, poignant division, marked by piano arpeggios and singing lyricism in the solo violin with answering passages in the quartet, soon gives way to a tremendous climax that marks the return of the first theme—a cry of utter desolation. This time the chromatic figure is in the strings, while the piano pours out the despairing theme. A short coda of sustained, slowly rising chords in the strings above the descending, still-rocking piano figure brings this powerful movement to a close.

The final movement, *très animé*, is full of driving energy and vitality. The piano begins the proceedings with the following theme, which rollicks and bounces along, soon joined by the other instruments. A variant follows in which syncopations play a prominent part. The piano announces a second theme in D major whose note values are longer. From time to time, the second theme of the *grave* returns, obeying the ground rules of cyclical form. The rollicking theme is presented in its original guise; there are some interesting short variations; and the movement comes to a triumphant con-clusion. Questions of form remain, however: is the movement an example of mostly variation form, as d'Indy asserts,[5] or is

Fig. 32. Chausson; Concert, 4, mm. 1–3

it a skillful combination of variation and rondo, with most of the emphasis on the latter? Surely the returns of the main theme in its essentially original form satisfy the requirements of rondo procedure, while the other material—including the cyclical theme—suggests the intervening episodes. Supporting the rondo solution to the problem is the almost *perpetuum mobile* spirit and tempo of much of the movement.

The Concert was dedicated to Eugène Ysaÿe—the first of two such dedications, the second being *Poème*—and was premiered in Brussels on March 4, 1892, with Ysaÿe and the young Parisian pianist Auguste Pierret in the solo spots; the Crickboom Quartet performed the remaining parts. Mathieu Crickboom, to whom Chausson was to dedicate his String Quartet, Op. 35, was a Belgian violinist then twenty-one years old, who with Pablo Casals later founded a quartet in Barcelona. Pierret was a substitute pianist, found by Pierre de Bréville to replace the scheduled one, who suddenly decided the part was too difficult. In gratitude for his outstanding performance, Chausson dedicated his next chamber work, the Piano Quartet, Op. 30, to him. The premiere was a resounding success, and Maurice Kufferath in *Le Guide Musical* referred to Chausson as "an ingenious inventor of new sonorities."[6]

Many of Chausson's happiest and most triumphant moments were associated with Brussels and the Belgian performers like Ysaÿe, Crickboom, and Désiré Demest who, as we saw, first sang *Poème de l'amour et de la mer.* Perhaps the guiding light in Brussel's progressive attitude toward all of the arts was Octave Maus, whom Chausson was most fortunate to have as a close friend and champion. Besides being an art critic, he was the founder in 1884 of the *Salon des XX,* which later became the Libre Esthétique. This institution was the principal center for exhibitions of Art Nouveau, but its gallery, "temporarily turned into a concert hall, displayed not only the freshly painted canvases of Pissarro, Renoir, Gauguin, and Signac, together with posters of Toulouse-Lautrec, but William Morris's illuminated books of the Kelmscott Press, Aubrey Beardsley's illustrations for Oscar Wilde's *Salomé,* and buckles and bracelets designed by the London Guild of Handicraft."[7] It was here that the Concert was first heard, together with two Fauré works. Artistically, Brussels' climate was certainly warmer and more disposed to new works than that of Paris, for not only was the Concert received enthusiastically by both the public and critics, but other Chausson works like *Viviane* and *La Tempête,* although not premiered in Brussels, received warm reviews not accorded them by Parisian critics. No wonder Chausson felt such an affinity for Belgium and Belgian artists!

In comparison with the passionately romantic and rhapsodic style of Concert, much of the Piano Quartet in A major, Op. 30, displays a cool, restrained, almost crisp style that leans towards the classic; it has already been noted in other works of 1896 and 1897 such as *Quelques danses* and *Vêpres du commun des vierges.* This is not to say that all traces of Chausson's earlier romantic fullness are absent here, for there are rhapsodic passages. However, the predominant style is more like that just mentioned, more what we have come to accept as typically French. It is in works like this that the truth of the oft-repeated statement that Chausson is a connecting link between Franck and Debussy becomes plain.

The crisp restraint can be heard from the outset of the first movement's jaunty main theme, marked *animé,* and declaimed by the piano (Figure 33). This theme shows traces

Fig. 33. Chausson; Piano Quartet, 1, mm. 1–4

of pentatonicism to at least the same degree as the majority of examples included in Brailoïu's study of this characteristic in Debussy. Its descending fourths are identical with those of the latter's *mélodie,* "Chevaux de bois" from *Ariettes oubliées,* cited by Brailoïu in his article. Of more interest than the pentatonic traits of each theme, however, are the reminiscences of *Parsifal* that Brailoïu and Gallois claim for their respective composers' fourths.[8] It is true, of course, that the latter, even rhythmically, are the same as Wagner's descending figure that so eloquently portrays the solemnity of the Grail Temple bells in Acts 1 and 3; but in view of the vast dissimilarities in purpose and tempo between the intervals as employed by the two composers and Wagner, it seems far-fetched to point out such resemblances. There is a whole family of themes that begins the same way, two other members of which are the chorale from Franck's *Prelude, Chorale, and Fugue,* and the theme with which Mahler's First Symphony opens (allowing in each of the latter for a minor rather than a major second between the second and third notes). It is the Franck theme to which Gallois refers and with which he couples Chausson's fourths when he cites Wagner as the fountainhead for both. If there must be comparisons between the materials employed by composers, it is absolutely essential that differences in intent, context, and the like be pointed out; otherwise injustices are done and perpetuated to the extent that generations of students and average listeners continue to accept uncritically such similarities as "influences," to the detriment of the "derivative" composer. We need very much to return to the older concept of the conscious or unconscious borrowing of musical material that is in a syntax common to a whole milieu of composers, one in which such borrowing is not considered as weakness or dependency *provided* the borrower uses such material in a novel and engaging manner. Viewed in this way and with the above standard rigidly applied, many composers' passages, including some of Chausson's, begin to live a life of their own with some dignity. This is certainly true with regard to the first theme of Chausson's Piano Quartet, where the chamber texture, the eighth-note figure on the second beat, and the fast tempo militate strongly against associations with *Parsifal.*

There is a great difference, of course, between the use of melodic material whose rhythms and intervallic contours are substantially the same for a whole generation of composers and the sudden appearance in a composer's music of passages that jolt the hearer into an instantaneous awareness of the same but more original passages in the music of another, better-known composer. This second type of similarity has already been pointed out several times in the course of this study of Chausson's music, notably in several songs and in the Symphony, where the references to Franck and Wagner constitute seemingly almost exact quotations. Such passages should not be condoned, certainly; but neither should they be condemned as plagiarism, for they appear, rather, as weaknesses in a composer's musical character.

Two more Chausson passages that fall into the second category occur in the first movement of the Piano Quartet. The first one is, again, strongly pentatonic, and reminds one of the similarly pentatonic melody in the first movement of the Symphony. It also bears a family resemblance to a passage from the first movement of Debussy's String Quartet; although the melodic contours are different, the rhythmic patterns and the use of repeated notes are identical, and they outline the melodies in the same fashion. Although not so close to being an exact quotation as some of the passages previously considered, it is a first cousin. Both passages appear in Figure 34; the Debussy excerpt appears in Brailoiu's study as Example 50.

Fig. 34. Chausson; Piano Quartet, 1, mm. 143–46
Debussy; String Quartet, 1, mm. 185–87

The second passage—Chausson's second theme—is more than just casually similar to the main theme of the first movement of Debussy's Quartet; the basic melodic contours and

rhythms are substantially the same (Figure 35). The same
Chausson melody, in A, harmonized in exactly the same
way, was apparently intended as the first theme of another
Concert for piano, oboe, viola, and string quartet; this project, dated September 1897, never materialized beyond
some sketches.[9] After this similar beginning, Chausson's
theme proceeds quite differently from Debussy's, and it is
clear that its composer had very different goals in mind as
to the use of his material for, as the movement progresses,
Chausson's harmonic writing is a mixture of diatonicism
and chromaticism from which all of the important features
of Debussy's style are absent. The emphasis appears to be
on essentially diatonic themes that can be chromatically
altered and harmonized in a developmental sense. This
latter process is not restricted to the development section,
for it occurs in other sections of the movement. Also present
is the technique, used earlier in the Symphony, of retaining
the diatonic character of the themes and creating plateaus
in which all or merely parts of the themes are heard; the

Fig. 35. Chausson; Piano Quartet, 1, mm. 89–90
Debussy; String Quartet, 1, mm. 1–2

plateaus are then connected by chromatic passages. From this process a certain amount of sequential writing results.

The second movement of Chausson's Piano Quartet, marked *très calme,* is a songlike piece in ternary form whose principal theme is announced by the viola. The second theme, more restless, contains much chromatic modulation of the tension-building kind, preparing the listener for the emotional high point at the return of the opening melody. Throughout the movement, the unhurried triple meter is never disturbed by any unusual rhythmic figures. The chords used to harmonize the eloquent melodies range from diatonic to chromatic; most of the latter are drawn from the vocabulary of late Romantic usage, and include various kinds of sevenths, ninths, and altered chords.

For his third movement Chausson has again chosen a songlike melody in triple meter. Marked *simple et sans hâte,* this movement is very different from its predecessor. D'Indy remarks that its main theme "seems to be constructed, thematically, on some folk song."[10] In view of Chausson's personal folklore collection, about which one would like to know much more, this is not surprising. Also, as is usual with many folk melodies, the theme is modal—in this instance transposed Phrygian (Figure 36). Chausson's subsequent treatment preserves the theme's essential modality, but in

Fig. 36. Chausson; Piano Quartet, 3, mm. 1–2

a tonal context in which almost continuous modulation is the norm. However, these modulations have the appearance of being spontaneous, as opposed to the carefully planned tonal schemes found in Franck. From time to time, as the material is assigned to the piano or the violin, the syncopated pizzicati act as a sort of framework in a most charming manner, the whole effect with its eighth-note movement being that of a light and rather elegant but not too fast scherzo. Early in the movement a short whole-tone passage in the violin temporarily evokes a Debussyan atmosphere.

The fourth movement, *animé,* gives us more substantial fare. It is a skillful combination of sonata and cyclic forms. The somewhat modal atmosphere of the first theme is brought about by the repeated use of the lowered second degree of the minor scale; it is also heightened by the frequent contrast between the lowered and the normal second. The second theme is more interesting because of its whole-tone construction as well as the fact that in its first presentation by the piano the material appears in each hand, separated by an octave; such parallelism is, of course, a Debussy characteristic, as is the whole-tone construction. Chausson's theme (Figure 37) is cyclical, having served as the second theme of the first movement. However, a comparison of the two appearances shows that in the fourth movement the theme has been altered to

Fig. 37. Chausson; Piano Quartet, 4, mm. 103–7

such an extent that a basic transformation rather than a simple restatement has occurred (see Figure 35). In this instance Chausson is not employing Franck's literal repetition of cyclical themes but is echoing Debussy's concept of cyclical form where, in the latter's Quartet, the same theme appears in all four movements, transformed in content and character. The remainder of Chausson's fourth movement is more conventional with regard to cyclical construction, for there is a long development followed by a recapitulation in which the other cyclic themes return more literally.

Rhythmically, throughout much of this fourth movement, there is a freedom and flexibility noticeably lacking in the preceding movements. Most of it is brought about by cross rhythms of various kinds between the piano and strings; these go beyond the simple juxtaposition of triplets against eighths heard in parts of the earlier movements. One is reminded of the cross rhythms that are so much a part of the second movement of Debussy's Quartet; the $\frac{6}{8}$ meter common to both strengthens the impression, and the patterns employed in each instance are very similar.

The unfinished String Quartet in C minor, Op. 35, consists of three movements. Dedicated to Crickboom, it was first performed by Parent, Lammers, Denayer, and Baretti at the Société Nationale on January 27, 1900. The concluding seventy-three measures of the third-movement scherzo were written by d'Indy from the composer's sketches and at the request of his family. In d'Indy's article on Chausson's chamber music, we are told that the Quartet stopped on the forty-eighth page of the Durand et Fils score. The account continues with d'Indy's remarks as to how he brought the movement to a close:

Having undertaken to complete the unfinished quartet, so as to make its performance practicable, I thought that it would not violate the ideas of my dead friend if I were to end this movement, begun in the subdominant, by a return to the principal key of the work. Making use, there-

fore, of a few indications very shortly sketched by the
composer, I reconstructed in the key of C Major what
Chausson would probably have written in F Major, in-
tending to write a finale. If this can be considered as a
fault, I alone must bear the responsibility.[11]

The first movement is in sonata form, preceded by a *grave*
introduction whose extremely serious theme, announced by
the cello, contains the germ for the first theme of the *allegro.*
Strangely enough, the shadow of Franck looms here at the
very moment one might have thought it dispelled in view
of the many preceding works where no traces of it can be
found. It is very evident in the two-measure sequential construction, as well as in the contour of the theme itself (Figure
38). Another short passage strongly reminiscent of Franck's

Fig. 38. Chausson; String Quartet, 1, mm. 1–5

methods is found at the very end of the exposition, where
the *grave* theme returns, set off by rests from the preceding
and following measures. Similar passages are frequent in
Franck's organ music, the pauses being necessitated by the
physical exertion connected with the pushing in and pulling
out of stops to effect changes in the tonal color. Such pauses
also appear in Franck's orchestral and chamber music—
perhaps an unconscious extension of the practice.

A large part of the development and recapitulation is concerned with a triplet figure derived from the slow introduction; unfortunately, it appears to function as filler material,
almost as though the music were marking time at the moment because there was nothing better for the instruments
to play and no particular goal in view. Much of the overly
sequential writing of the movement centers around this
figure, and the steadily mounting excitement thus generated
becomes less and less effective because the rise in emotional
temperature seems to lack motivation. Several passages
where two or three of the instruments participate in the
triplet figure remind one of similar places in the first movement of Debussy's Quartet. There the triplet figure is also
filler material and does not really contribute to the organic
structure of the movement. Both quartets suffer—at least
in their first movements—from not having sufficient independence in the individual parts, no matter how effective
the ensemble sound may be.

The second movement—a short, songlike slow piece in
ternary form—is much better than the first with respect to
independence of parts. The second theme is more memorable than the first, and is shared more extensively by the
four instruments. It undergoes a certain amount of development in which the head motive, a descending triad, is severed
for a short while from the rest of the theme and put through
some rhythmic variations. The writing throughout the movement is purposeful and sure; and although neither melody
can be called distinguished, interest is maintained by the
sharing of the material and the spotlight thrown on the
individual instruments from time to time as parts cross. In
short, the movement is well written and affords very pleasant
listening.

Perhaps the third movement was on Chausson's mind
when, in a letter of July 12, 1898, in which he informed
Crickboom that he was working on a string quartet for him,
he expressed his fear that the quartet stemmed "rather di-

rectly from Beethoven."[12] This statement, while correct, need not have caused Chausson any discomfiture or shame, for his well-made and exciting *scherzo* shows clearly the superior direction in which the composer was obviously moving, based on sound techniques he had absorbed from Beethoven. The model, almost certainly, was the *scherzando vivace* of Op. 127. The external similarities are, of course, the most apparent: the triple meters of each movement, and the rhythmic figures with which both composers are concerned throughout large areas of each movement (Figure 39). Another outward resemblance is the sudden tempo

Fig. 39. Chausson; String Quartet, 3, mm. 5–8
Beethoven; Quartet, Op. 127, 3, mm. 2–5

changes for a few measures before resumption of the original tempo or the adoption of a new one. This characteristic is, of course, frequently encountered throughout many of Beethoven's last works—piano sonatas as well as string quartets.

Of far greater moment, however, than these externals

themselves is the use to which Chausson puts them in his overall plan. Here, in the last music he was ever to write, he sought like the Beethoven of the final creative period to realize all of the inherent possibilities of his thematic material; and it is precisely in this area that his observations and probable studies of Beethovenian techniques benefited him greatly and pointed the way to the future—a future that, tragically, never materialized. The initial four-note rhythmic motive at the head of the F minor theme with which the movement begins, and from which the descending figure in measure 2 is derived by virtue of the opening minor second (Figure 40), is subjected to a number of intervallic

Fig. 40. Chausson; String Quartet, 3, mm. 1-2

changes and partial, though free, inversion. The descending figure is similarly treated (Figure 39 shows a variant in which inversion is featured). All of the variants, whether of the initial four notes or the descending figure, are distributed freely throughout all four strings, resulting in a complex fabric where two variants may be present at the same time. This boisterous, good-natured section marked *gaiment et pas trop vite,* with its often disjunct movement, gives way to a quiet part in which an admirably contrasted theme—soft and conjunct—is heard. The key is now E major, and the meter is $\frac{2}{4}$. Chausson has created a balance between both sections to the degree that where the angular first theme with its components contains every type of variant except rhythmic, the second theme (except for small alterations) retains its essential melodic shape but is subjected to rhythmic changes. These last are effected in rather large segments, so that there is a sense of mounting tension and climax as the theme progresses from sixteenths to triplets; then faster triplets (*plus vite*); and finally $\frac{5}{8}$ (*encore plus vite*), where the pounding eighth-note movement is marked *forte* and *staccato.* The progression is not without interruption, for between the first group of triplets and the faster second group, the angular *gaiment* section intervenes, preceded by three measures of the opening material in slow tempo—an interlude similar to those often found in late Beethoven. The $\frac{5}{8}$ section is joined without a break to the preceding *plus vite* duple movement, and is the concluding part written by d'Indy. Just before the final page, another Beethovenian slow interruption occurs, in which the first theme of the movement is heard. Then comes a return to the headlong pace, followed by a reminder in augmentation of the first theme. In the final d'Indy section, there are several meter changes.

Although d'Indy mentioned in the remarks, cited earlier, that he made use of "a few indications very shortly sketched by the composer," it can be assumed that these sketches were complete enough for the movement to be finished in accordance with the composer's wishes, except for the transposition of Chausson's concluding material from a probable F to C major. Although d'Indy's reasons for the key change are understandable, having been motivated by the natural desire to end the unfinished quartet in the tonic major, the alteration seems unfortunate, for the subdominant major is an integral part of the total structure. The latter was obviously planned very carefully, and here again Beethoven's *scherzando vivace* of Op. 127 was a possible model. Chausson's structural design reveals a *scherzo* wherein the second theme functions as a trio; after the return of the *scherzo* in the initial key, the second theme—this time *plus vite* and in triplets—serves as a second trio. Following this, the *scherzo* fails to return, as we have seen, except for the very briefest moment at the very end; and the trio section in its *encore plus vite* tempo and asymmetrical meter brings the movement to a close. The tension engendered by the fast and yet faster tempi of the trio gives the unmistakable impression that Chausson wished the second idea to dominate. The ground plan thus becomes

A	B	A	B
F minor	E major	F minor	C major-F major
			C major (d'Indy)

At first sight, Beethoven's design seems the same. His *scherzo* concerns itself with the cell motive (Figure 39), while the trio is an extremely rapid *presto*; the *scherzo* is repeated, but just after the *presto* resumes, it is abruptly cut off by directions compelling the players to jump to the coda, where the cell motive is briefly heard. The whole movement, as well as Beethoven's termination of the *presto*, is an example of the gruff humor associated with this composer, and we cannot expect Chausson to follow suit; such tactics were not in his nature. However, the thematic resemblance between the little cells, the tempo changes, and the near similarities in structure (but for Beethoven's joke, the plans would be almost identical) confirm Chausson's reference in his letter of July 12, 1898, to his great predecessor. Beethoven *was* consulted, but the study produced one of the most workmanlike and exciting movements to be found in Chausson.

Further corroboration of Chausson's familiarity with the string quartets of Beethoven is provided by Barricelli and Weinstein where, after their catalogue of Chausson's works, six selected Beethoven quartet movements appear in a short list of transcriptions, although no mention is made concerning the medium for which Chausson transcribed them.[13] Each of the movements is from a different quartet, and the six quartets range from Op. 18, no. 1 to Op. 135; Op. 127 is not among them.

In point of time, *Pièce*, for violoncello (or viola) and piano, Op. 39, was composed in August 1897, and thus came into being during the writing of the Piano Quartet, Op. 30. It was written over a year before the completion of the first movement of the String Quartet, Op. 35, yet it bears the final opus number in Chausson's total production. It is a short, one-movement work without any pretense to profundity, and therein lies its charm. It is most engagingly written for each instrument. As still another example of Chausson's late style, its essential classicism is emphasized by a carefully balanced and well-proportioned structure, as well as by thematic material in most of which a certain detachment and reserve are noticeable.

From the structural viewpoint, *Pièce* is a short rondo whose individual sections differ from each other with respect to instrumental dominance. In Section A's twenty-two measures, the material is shared at the beginning, but the cello soon adopts a subordinate role. The situation is reversed in the *plus animé* of Section B, where for fourteen measures the cello holds forth with its own new melody while the piano provides syncopated chords as a harmonic foundation. The recurrence of A (really an A') is very brief; its six measures are restricted to the piano while the cello plays a broad passage against it. The remaining ten measures before the appearance of Section C are taken up with transitional material. With the arrival of Section C, the new material is shared equally by the two instruments, the piano part featuring sixteenths in which the new melody is embedded. This section is the warmest and most emotional of *Pièce* to the degree that the classical restraint is abandoned. After a steady crescendo, the concluding A'' section is stated *fortissimo, plus large* in the piano. Six measures of transition lead to a quiet restatement of the opening material in the piano while the cello sings some of its Section B melody.

Rhythmically, *Pièce* is quite unusual. Except for ten measures of $\frac{4}{4}$ meter, it is in $\frac{5}{4}$ and $\frac{7}{4}$ meter throughout. And just as carefully as Chausson has balanced the instrumental participation in the various sections, so has he considered the rhythmic distribution. The ten measures of $\frac{4}{4}$ occur as the transition in Section A', almost exactly in the center. They are flanked by forty-two measures of $\frac{5}{4}$ from the beginning to that point, and by thirty-nine measures from there to the end (all of Section C and the first ten measures of A'' are in $\frac{7}{4}$) of $\frac{7}{4}$ and $\frac{5}{4}$. Nor is this all, for Chausson has divided each of the $\frac{5}{4}$ segments into 2 plus 3, and the $\frac{7}{4}$ segment into 4 plus 3; dotted lines through each full measure make his intentions clear.

Structure, of course, exists only as the basic framework of a piece of creative art, and no amount of care taken in its formulation can guarantee an interesting result if the subject matter itself is not interesting and appealing. In *Pièce*, Chausson's material is attractive with—in the first theme— a charming turn of phrase supported by simple harmonies; the resulting flavor is somewhat antique (Figure 41). The

Fig. 41. Chausson; *Pièce*, mm. 1–2

remainder of the thematic material is more conventional, but in each instance it contrasts well with the recurring melody. Thus Chausson's classicism at the end of his life was not merely a matter of lowered emotional temperature, but concerned structural balance in which melodies, rhythms and sonorities were carefully planned and weighed against one another. The result in *Pièce* is a work that should become a permanent part of the cello literature. *Pièce* is fully as satisfying as the well-known *Elégie* of Fauré, composed in 1883 for cello and piano but later orchestrated and heard today almost exclusively in that form. The two works are admirably contrasted, for they inhabit different emotional worlds; yet their lengths are about the same. Including them on the same program would be an interesting way of showing these contrasts and demonstrating the superior qualities of each.

NOTES

1. Quoted in Barricelli and Weinstein, *Ernest Chausson*, p. 49.

2. Gallois, *Ernest Chausson*, p. 45.

3. Barricelli and Weinstein, *Ernest Chausson*, p. 49n.

4. Gallois, *Ernest Chausson*, p. 157.

5. Vincent d'Indy, "Ernest Chausson," *Cyclopedic Survey of Chamber Music*, comp. and ed. Walter Willson Cobbett, 2d ed. (London: Oxford University Press, 1963), 1:267.

6. Quoted in Gallois, *Ernest Chausson*, p. 178.

7. Lockspeiser, *Debussy: His Life and Mind*, 1:119.

8. Brailoïu, *Pentatony in Debussy's Music*, p. 399; Jean Gallois, *César Franck* (Paris: Éditions de Seuil, 1966), p. 146.

9. Barricelli and Weinstein, *Ernest Chausson*, p. 149n.

10. d'Indy, "Ernest Chausson," *Cyclopedic Survey of Chamber Music*, 1:268.

11. Ibid., 270.

12. Gallois, *Ernest Chausson*, p. 68. This assertion followed immediately his view that the work was "neither Franck, nor d'Indy, nor Debussy," thereby confirming his awareness of possible influences from these quarters. As we have seen, however, the first movement does contain references to Franck and Debussy.

13. Barricelli and Weinstein, *Ernest Chausson*, p. 226.

_____ 7 _____

Miscellaneous Works

L IKE most composers, Chausson wrote works from time to time that do not fit any of the larger categories we have thus far considered. In his case, all such remaining works share a common denominator: they are all choral or vocal. Neither group is large enough or of sufficient importance to warrant a chapter of its own, although if all of the religious music—choral and vocal—had been published, a strong argument for separate status could be advanced.

Ten accompanied motets—two without opus number, the rest comprising three opus numbers—form the corpus of Chausson's religious music.[1] The two unnumbered motets need not detain us: the first is "O Salutaris" and dates from 1879, while the second, "Tantum ergo," was composed in 1891. Both remain unpublished. The first two of the remaining eight, "Deus Abraham" and "Ave Verum," constitute Op. 6, and were scored for solo voice, violin, and organ; only the second of these has been published. Although they are not quite student works, having been written in September 1883, some months after Chausson had completed his studies with Franck, they contain nothing significant or memorable. In fact, Gallois speaks of the "facture banale" of "Ave Verum."[2]

In 1886 Chausson composed the three motets of Op. 12: "Ave Maria," "Tota pulchra es," and "Ave Maris Stella." Only the second motet has been published; it is scored for solo soprano and piano, organ, or harmonium, although the concluding four measures are augmented by a quiet, four-part choral *amen*. As might be expected, the prayerful setting is marked *assez lent*. There are no dynamic indications of any kind, yet it is obvious that a soft, calm atmosphere is intended. The thematic material is simple and the supporting, often chromatic, harmonies are generally effective; occasionally, however, the chromaticism seems excessive and unmotivated.

The last set of three motets constitutes Op. 16, and is composed of "Lauda Sion" (1888), "Benedictus" (1890), and "Pater noster" (1891). Only the final one has been published and, like "Tota pulchra es," is for soprano solo and keyboard accompaniment. On the whole it is more successful than the last named, for its chromaticism is better managed. It is also more subjective than its predecessor, a result brought about by tensions caused by the chromatic texture and the sense of climax at the end. Each motet has an entirely different expressive goal, of course: "Tota pulchra es" is an objective, quiet prayer, while "Pater noster" has a certain anguished sense of urgency. But if we allow for these differences, the writing in the later motet is less forced and more masterly, allowing the expressive goal to be more skillfully and naturally attained. The first performance in 1892 failed to impress at least one critic, judging from the following scathing review: "As for the *Pater Noster* of M.E. Chausson, we shall wish that this first performance may be the last, and we shall pity the singer, M. Maugière, for having been mixed up with this empty and pretentious music. . . ."[3]

It seems strange indeed that the one work Chausson dedicated to César Franck was not one of his important, multi-movement orchestral or chamber music compositions. These are types for which Franck was well-known and in which he excelled, and one might suppose that a dedication would be in an area wherein Chausson sensed a kinship or felt an obligation with respect to what he had learned and absorbed from his former teacher. The only other dedication to a

recognized composer is to Chausson's fellow Franckist
Henri Duparc, and the work—*Poème de l'amour et de la
mer*—implies a musical kinship in the realm of the *mélodie*.
Perhaps Chausson, for whom the act of composing was a
struggle in most instances, was too lacking in self-confidence
to dedicate a major work to Franck, the hub and *raison
d'être* of the entire circle that revolved around him.

Whatever the reasons for the existing dedication may be,
the music with which Franck was honored is a choral work,
now totally unknown—*Hymne védique*, Op. 9, composed in
January and February of 1886 and written for four-part
mixed chorus, soprano and contralto soli, and orchestra.
The text, by Leconte de Lisle, is based on Hindu religious
thought and is in the form of a prayer to a Hindu deity
in which evil, death, and final liberation are the subjects.
One cannot help wondering what Franck's interest in such
a text might have been. True, the problem of Good and
Evil was one of his favorite themes (*Rédemption, Les Béatitudes, Le Chasseur maudit*), but from a Christian viewpoint.
Whether he had read or was familiar with non-Christian
points of view is debatable.

Despite the dedication to Franck, the music of *Hymne
védique* is not Franckian at all, but superficially Wagnerian
with respect to Chausson's lavish use of the *Tristan* Chord
which, in the chorus parts, is found fourteen times; in the
orchestral accompaniment the number is thirty-four. In view
of the twenty-two-page length of the work (piano-vocal
score), this is a high incidence; yet neither text nor emotional
considerations appear to have entered into its use. Most of
the harmony of *Hymne védique* is concerned with almost
continuous transitions and modulations in which the *Tristan*
Chord serves in either a decorative capacity or as a factor in
the transitions and modulations. Still, the overall effect of
the work is not Wagnerian, in spite of the *Tristan* Chords,
because the subtleties brought about by Wagner's use of
suspensions and appoggiaturas—so often a result of interior

voice-leading—are conspicuously missing. Instead of the liquid flow of individual voice parts, most of the choral writing is block-like; at times it is also dramatically powerful. As for its premiere, *Hymne védique* had the misfortune to be performed at the Société Nationale on the same April day in 1887 that was chosen for the French premiere of *Lohengrin* at the Eden Theatre. The work does not deserve the oblivion into which it has fallen ever since.

Finally, three works whose tranquil and serene moods are somewhat rare in Chausson's emotional world are the *Deux Duos*, Op. 11, for two female voices; and *Chant nuptial*, Op. 15, for four-part women's choir. The first of the duos, *La Nuit* (1883), is to a text by the Parnassian poet Théodore de Banville; while the second, *Le Réveil* (1886), has a text by Balzac. Both of these short pieces possess a simple charm that mirrors the naturalness of the texts. A third duet, *Chanson de noces dans les bois*, after a Lithuanian song by André Theuriet, carries a penciled notation, "Op. 11, no. 3"; however, it was never published. The *Chant nuptial*, delicate and almost religious in its serenity, is a setting of Leconte de Lisle's ode to marriage.

Notes

1. Although *Les Vêpres du commun des vierges* for organ is sometimes considered as a work of sacred music—a conclusion obviously reached by virtue of its Gregorian origins (both Gallois and Barricelli and Weinstein treat it in this context)—its medium as well as its attractiveness for recital purposes dictate that it be placed in the realm of keyboard music (see chap. 4).

2. Gallois, *Ernest Chausson*, p. 111.

3. Ibid., p. 177.

8

Epilogue

IT is almost inevitable that the study of a neglected artist must appear to some readers to make over-generous claims for its subject; yet the undertaking would certainly be unjustified but for the conviction that opportunities to know the artist by direct experience would bring many toward the present enthusiasm of the few. This study has not claimed that Chausson, highly self-critical and then deprived of his life at an age when most composers attain artistic maturity, should be placed in the same rank as Wagner or Debussy. However, before reaching the conclusions proper to an epilogue, let us summarize the claims made in the preceding chapters.

Chausson was so often in masterly command of the setting of French texts and the appropriate role of the accompaniment that many of his *mélodies* are entitled to be ranked at or near the top of the genre; his Symphony in B-flat major and his opera *Le Roi Arthus*, despite unavoidable re-semblances to the achievements of Franck and Wagner in these respective fields, are more strongly individual works than critics up to now have seen fit to acknowledge; his *Poème* is a carefully constructed and emotionally moving work of high inspiration; his two major works for keyboard— *Quelques danses* and *Les Vêpres du commun des vierges*— are highly deserving of greater recognition, both as to musical quality and as important contributions in progressive and restorative movements; and finally, certain chamber works like Concert in D major for piano, violin, and string quartet are as emotionally powerful as many other works in the standard repertory.

One further and important conclusion has helped unwittingly to dictate the separate conclusions just enumerated. It is the ultimate answer to a problem with which we were partially concerned in the first chapter: Chausson's position in and relationship to the culture of his time. We looked at this question with respect to Camille Mauclair's portrayal of him in the novel *Le Soleil des morts*, where he appeared to occupy a central position between the two extremes then prevalent in French literary circles: Symbolist passivity and inaction represented by Mallarmé, and the feverish, revolutionary activity associated with Zola. In my discussion, I postulated the theory that Mauclair's dedication of the book to Chausson and the explicit noninvolvement of Chausson in any of the novel's events and arguments were designed to imply a neutral position, or perhaps a place above the battle lines. When this theory is reduced to more manageable proportions with respect to Chausson's achievements as a composer by substituting Wagner's musical revolution for the literary radicalism of Zola, the musical analyses reveal a constant struggle between the delicate intimations and suggestions associated with Symbolist aesthetics and the overstatements and exaggerations of the Wagnerian aesthetic. The artistic principles of the Symbolists are essentially French, whereas those of Wagner are characteristically German; and one should infer from this that those Chausson works which adhere more closely to the French point of view are more successful. Thus a *mélodie* like the setting of Verlaines's *La Lune blanche (Apaisement)* is more effective in its simplicity and understatement than *Printemps triste*, with its heavy Wagnerian harmonies pushed to over-repetitive limits. This statement should, of course, be understood in the context of Chausson's nationality; he was, after all, a Frenchman, who from time to time strayed across the musical border. Chronology has little or nothing to do with the problem, for until the end of his life, when he adopted a more classical approach, there is no accounting for the sudden shifts in style from understatement to overemphasis, nor in them is there any discernible pattern. A typically French *mélodie* may be preceded or followed by an elaborate setting in which the harmonies of the accompaniment are heavily chromatic in their complications, although the vocal line may be (and usually is) utterly faithful, in an understated manner, to the textual nuances.

Although the later analyst and critic may feel that Chausson's understated musical language is more appropriate and successful than the repetitive overstatements, the average critic and listener of the composer's own time disagreed, as Laurence Davies points out:

A standard criticism of his music was expressed in the comment of one unfavourable observer who likened it to "stew without meat". Even after the second—and unquestionably more successful—presentation of his symphony by Nikisch and the Berlin Philharmonic, the press still thought fit to attack him as "the Mallarmé of music". This might have been interpreted as a compliment had it sprung from really informed sources. Unfortunately, all it reflected was the enormous public ignorance surrounding matters of aesthetic theory. The delicate presentiments contained in the work of men like Chausson and Mallarmé simply failed to penetrate the average hidebound sensibility. People were taught to appreciate only what was concrete and unequivocal.[1]

Today we seem to be experiencing the opposite problem: any resemblances to Franck and Wagner are singled out for derisive comment. Davies brings this contradiction to our attention when he says, "it is true that the word 'restrained' was frequently used in a derogatory sense about his work [again, during the composer's lifetime], but this hardly chimes with the current opinion that it suffers from too many 'swooning' phrases."[2]

Let us return to the original question of Chausson's position in the culture of his time. Mauclair's estimate—if one is accurate in judging it to be illustrative of a kind of neutral centrality—is equivalent to an idealization that is not supported by the facts. This is not to say that Chausson allowed himself to be swayed by all of the conflicting winds of his era, but given his intellectual curiosity concerning the various artistic movements swirling around him—Symbolism and Naturalism in literature, Impressionism and the Nabi train of thought in art—it would be very disappointing to see him uninvolved. One cannot imagine that the brilliant guest list at 22 Boulevard de Courcelles could possibly leave him unaffected. True, Mauclair portrayed him as having "always the appearance of rising from the middle of a dream and taking a step toward real life,"[3] but at least he *did* take that step. His preferences for retreating to the privacy of his large and luxuriously appointed study and fleeing from the noise and disturbances of Paris are in no way synonymous with negation or neutrality. They simply provided him with the means for greater mental concentration. That he did withdraw into himself is no doubt true, but he always seemed to emerge successfully and, as time went on, his self-doubts and hesitations became less evident. Considering Chausson's late start in music, the doubts that resulted from that final decision, and the natural shyness and sensitivity with which he was endowed, it is a wonder that he accomplished as much as he did. He could easily have retreated into his wealth and weakly dabbled. Had he chosen to do so, he would not have been the subject for this or any other book.

For a final estimate of Chausson's music, we need to reconcile ourselves to the inescapable fact that the two polarities discussed above do exist, together with works that mix elements of each; *Poème de l'amour et de la mer* is a good example. Only when we accept this premise will we recognize that we are in the presence of an important transitional style between the idioms of Franck and Debussy. That

Chausson was aware that he was possibly drifting away from the rigors of the Franck school seems implicit in his reply to a Debussy letter of October 1893, in which Debussy warned him against being preoccupied with "undertones." Chausson's reply acknowledged that Debussy was correct, and went on to say:

> While you were writing me I thought just about the same thing, the beginning of my third act [of *Le Roi Arthus*] proves that. I believe I owe that preoccupation especially to the *Société Nationale*. Its concerts resemble oftentimes a kind of doctoral examination. You have to prove that you know your craft. That is a great error; doubtless knowing one's craft is necessary, but it is still more indispensable to have one's individual craft. A work of art is not a thesis and in it skill should never be anything but a secondary quality. All that does not deny that the *Société Nationale* has rendered great services and is still the place in Paris where we hear the best modern music. [4]

The detractors of Chausson never bother, of course, to print these revealing lines! All they see are the superficial resemblances. Careful listening will, however, reveal an attractive body of music that can and should be enjoyed on its own terms, without a search for greatness that it does not possess, or a constant criticism of it for what it does and does not contain.

NOTES

1. Davies, *César Franck and His Circle*, p. 192.
2. Ibid.
3. See chap. 1 for the discussion of this and other relevant points.
4. Quoted in Barricelli and Weinstein, *Ernest Chausson*, p. 67.

Appendixes

APPENDIX A

Catalogue of the Works of Ernest Chausson

Op. 1 *Cinq Fantaisies pour piano* (destroyed). 1879-80.

Op. 2 *Sept Mélodies*
Nanny (Leconte de Lisle) 1880
Le Charme (Armand Silvestre) 1879
Les Papillons (Théophile Gautier) 1880
La Dernière Feuille (Théophile Gautier) 1880
Sérénade italienne (Paul Bourget) 1882
Hébé (Louise Ackermann) 1882
Le Colibri (Leconte de Lisle) 1882

Op. 3 Trio in G minor for piano, violin, and cello 1881

Op. 4 *Les Caprices de Marianne*, lyrical comedy after Alfred de Musset. Unpublished. 1882-84

Op. 5 *Viviane*, symphonic poem after a legend of the Round Table. 1882

Op. 6 *Deux Motets* for solo voice, violin, and organ
Deus Abraham 1883
Ave Verum 1883

Op. 7 *Hélène*, lyrical drama in two acts after Leconte de Lisle. Unpublished except for a women's chorus with orchestra, and *Le Jugement de Paris*. 1883-86

Op. 8 *Quatre Mélodies* on poems of Maurice Bouchor
Nocturne 1886
Amour d'antan 1882
Printemps triste 1883-88
Nos Souvenirs 1888

Op. 9 *Hymne védique*, mixed chorus and orchestra. Text by Leconte de Lisle. 1886

Op. 10 *Solitude dans les bois*, symphonic poem (destroyed). 1886

Op. 11 *Deux Duos* for two female voices
 La Nuit (Théodore de Banville) 1883
 Le Réveil (Honoré de Balzac) 1886

Op. 12 *Trois Motets* for four mixed voices, cello, harp, and organ.
 Ave Maria 1886
 Tota pulchra es 1886
 Ave Maris Stella 1886
 Unpublished except for *Tota pulchra es*. The present available edition is scored for solo soprano, organ or harmonium, and a concluding four-measure mixed chorus.

Op. 13 *Quatre Mélodies*
 Apaisement (Paul Verlaine) 1885
 Sérénade (Jean Lahor) 1887
 L'Aveu (Villiers de l'Isle-Adam) 1887
 La Cigale (Leconte de Lisle) 1887

Op. 14 *La Caravane* (Théophile Gautier) 1887

Op. 15 *Chant nuptial*, four-part women's chorus. Text by Leconte de Lisle. 1887-88

Op. 16 *Trois Motets*
 Lauda Sion 1888
 Benedictus 1890
 Pater noster 1891
 Unpublished except for *Pater noster*. Scored for soprano solo and keyboard accompaniment.

Op. 17 *Chansons de Miarka* on poems of Jean Richepin
 Les Morts 1888
 La Pluie 1888

Op. 18 *La Tempête*, incidental music for Shakespeare's play in Maurice Bouchor's translation. Scored for small orchestra (one each of the following: flute, violin, harp, celesta) and voices. 1888
 Chant d'Ariel
 Air de danse
 Juno and Cérès
 Danse rustique
 Chanson d'Ariel

Op. 19 *Poème de l'amour et de la mer* (Maurice Bouchor)
 La Fleur des eaux 1882-90. Revised in 1893

Orchestral interlude
La Mort de l'amour 1887
The second *mélodie* has been published separately under the title of "Le Temps des lilas."

Op. 20 Symphony in B-flat major 1889-90

Op. 21 Concert in D major for piano, violin, and string quartet 1889-91

Op. 22 *La Légende de Sainte Cécile*, incidental music for the drama of Maurice Bouchor. Scored for soli, women's chorus, and small orchestra. 1891

Op. 23 *Le Roi Arthus*, opera in three acts and six tableaux. Libretto by the composer. 1886-95

Op. 24 *Serres chaudes* (Maurice Maeterlinck)
     Serre chaude 1896
     Serre d'ennui 1893
     Lassitude 1893
     Fauves las 1896
     Oraison 1895-96

Op. 25 *Poème*, for violin and orchestra 1896

Op. 26 *Quelques danses*, piano 1896
     Dédicace
     Sarabande
     Pavane
     Forlane

Op. 27 *Trois Lieder* (Camille Mauclair)
     Les Heures 1896
     Ballade 1896
     Les Couronnes 1896

Op. 28 *Chansons de Shakespeare* (translations by Maurice Bouchor)
     Chanson de clown (Twelfth Night) 1890
     Chanson d'amour (Measure for Measure) 1891
     Chanson d'Ophélie (Hamlet) 1896
     Chant funèbre (Much Ado About Nothing). Four-part women's choir and orchestra. 1897

Op. 29 *Ballata, a cappella* chorus of mixed voices after Dante. Unpublished. 1896-97

Op. 30 Quartet in A major for piano, violin, viola, and cello 1897

Op. 31 *Les Vêpres du commun des vierges*, organ 1897

Op. 32 *Soir de fête*, symphonic poem based on an idea of the composer's. Unpublished. 1897-98

Op. 33 *Pour un arbre de Noël, mélodie.* Unpublished. 1898

Op. 34 *Deux Poèmes de Verlaine*
La Chanson bien douce 1898
Le Chevalier malheur 1898

Op. 35 String Quartet in C minor (unfinished). Third movement completed by Vincent d'Indy. 1898-99

Op. 36 *Deux Mélodies*
Cantique à l'épouse (Albert Jounet) 1898
Dans la forêt du charme et de l'enchantement (Jean Moréas) 1898

Op. 37 *Chanson Perpétuelle* (Charles Cros). Scored for piano; orchestra; and a combination of piano and string quartet. 1898

Op. 38 *Paysage*, piano 1895

Op. 39 *Pièce*, for cello (or viola) and piano 1897

In addition to the above list, there are works—a substantial quantity—that lack opus numbers and remain unpublished. Most of these are student efforts; they appear below, arranged in chronological order.

Les Lilas, mélodie (Maurice Bouchor) 1877

Two Sonatinas for Piano (Four Hands); G minor, D minor 1878-79

Le Petit Sentier, mélodie (Maurice Bouchor) 1878

L'Albatros, mélodie (Charles Baudelaire) 1879

Le Rideau de ma voisine, mélodie (Alfred de Musset) 1879

O Salutaris, motet for solo voice and organ 1879

La Veuve du roi Basque, ballad for choruses, soli, and orchestra (Brethous-Lafargue) 1879

Hylas, fragment for chorus, soli, and orchestra after Leconte de Lisle. Probably 1879-80

Jeanne d'Arc, lyrical scene for solo voices and women's chorus (author unknown) 1879-80

Esméralda (Victor Hugo) Act 4, Scene 1 (two versions) 1880

Fugues on themes of Bach, Franck, Hasse, Massenet, Saint-Saëns 1880-81

Sonata in F minor, piano 1880

Hymne à la nature, mixed chorus and orchestra. Text by Armand Silvestre 1881

Andante and Allegro for clarinet with piano accompaniment 1881

L'Arabe, men's chorus, tenor solo, and orchestra (author unknown). Prix de Rome entry. 1881

Nous nous aimerons, mélodie (author unknown) 1882

Marche militaire, piano 1884

Le Mort maudit, mélodie (Jean Richepin) 1884

Chanson de noces dans les bois, after a Lithuanian song by André Theuriet. For two sopranos and piano. According to a penciled notation, the piece was intended to be included in Op. 11 (no. 3) 1885

Les Oiseaux, incidental music for Aristophanes' play. Scored for flute and harp. 1889

Tantum ergo, motet 1891

Concert for piano, oboe, viola, and string quartet (sketches) 1897

Symphony no. 2 (sketches) 1899

Two other unnumbered works—the *mélodies L'Ame des bois* and *Chanson*, composed in 1878 on poems of Bouchor—enjoy the distinction of having been published (by Durand).

APPENDIX B

Paintings from the Chausson Collection Sold by Mme Chausson
at Auction June 5, 1936

ARTIST	TITLE	AMOUNT
Carrière	*Portrait de femme*	2,000 fr.
	Tête de femme	410
	Le Baiser	2,300
Chintreuil	*Le Champ de trèfle*	1,520
Corot	*Rome, le parc et la villa Borghèse*	29,000
	Trouville; barque de pêche à marée basse	36,200
Degas	*Études de danseuse* (pastel)	4,600
	Danseuse (dessin au crayon noir)	6,100
	Le Bain (pastel)	18,000
	La Danseuse étoile (pastel)	29,000
	Danseuse au repos (pastel)	40,200
	La Danseuse aux bas rouges (pastel)	30,000
	Femme nue se coiffant (pastel)	76,000
	Les Blanchisseuses (pastel)	40,200
	Portrait d'homme (présumé le peintre Bellet-Dupoisat)	107,000
Delacroix	*Hamlet tente de tuer le roi* (dessin à la mine de plomb)	1,500
	Études de robes pour la Fiancée de Lammermoor, scene du contrat (aquarelle): and *Études de costumes et de manteaux masculins* pour la même scène (aquarelle et croquis à la mine de plomb)	430
	Lion couché dévorant une proie (dessin à la mine de plomb)	310
	Arabe à cheval chargeant, le sabre en main (dessin à la mine de plomb)	1,200
	*Études de Marocains (*dessin à la mine de plomb)	1,460
	Lion blessé, une patte levée (des-	700

	sin à la mine de plomb) et *Page de croquis: Lionne* (dessin à la mine de plomb)	
	Croquis d'hommes, de chevaux et de pattes (dessin à la mine de plomb) et *Étude de deux chevaux* (croquis à la mine de plomb)	1,120
	Étude d'une figure d'homme (dessin à la mine de plomb) et *Étude d'Arabe* (dessin à la mine de plomb)	450
	La Paix, descendant sur la terre, vient consoler les hommes et ramener l'abondance (esquisse)	16,000
École française	*Tivoli, les jardins de la Villa d'Este, XIX siècle*	1,200
	Groupe d'enfants dans un parc	1,050
Gauguin	*Un Pacage à la Martinique* (gouache en form d'éventail) et *Vue de la Martinique* (gouache en forme d'éventail), ensemble	16,000
Manet	*Marine, temps calme*	30,000
Morisot	*Sous la vérandah*	63,500
Puvis de Chavannes	*Orphée*	8,600
Renoir	*Le Chapeau de paille*	15,000
	Tête de fillette	27,000
Riesener	*Étude pour la Léda*	2,700
	Le Chateau de Chambord	500
Signac	*La Seine à Argenteuil, effet de soleil*	3,600

Total amount realized from sale 614,850 fr.

In addition to the above-named paintings, Chausson also owned the following: works by Bonnard; Courbet; Denis; Lerolle; Redon (*La Vierge d'Aurore*, oil; *L'Ange déchu*, charcoal); Renoir (*Portrait de son fils, Coco*); and Vuillard.

The family portraits constitute a special category: one by Besnard pictures the Chaussons at the piano; Carrière painted a portrait of Chausson, and also a family portrait; Denis painted *Mme Ernest Chausson et son fils Laurent, à Fiesole*; there is a portrait of Mme Chausson by Berthe Morisot; and a red chalk portrait of Chausson by Redon.

Chausson's mansion also contained decorations by Denis (three ceilings: *Avril, Le Printemps,* and *Terrase de Fiesole*); Lerolle; and Redon (five-section decorative screen in tempora for Mme Chausson's small music salon. Completed in 1902. Subject: plants).

APPENDIX C

Discography

It is gratifying to report that the situation with respect to re-corded performances of Chausson's music is slowly improving. A perusal of the following list will show that the two most important orchestral and the three principal chamber works are well rep-resented. The major piano works and two of the *mélodies* with orchestra are included, but it is regrettable that there are no recordings of the *mélodies* with piano accompaniment. It is possible, of course, that one or two of the latter may be included in a collection. An excellent recording of the symphonic poem *Viviane* (Almeida and the New Philharmonia, RCA LSC-3151), is, un-fortunately, no longer available.

All of the following items (with the exception of the Russian recording of the Concert) are included in the Schwann-1 catalogue for December 1977, *or* the 1978 Musical Heritage Society catalogue.

Chanson Perpétuelle, Op. 37 Janet Baker and the Melos Ensemble	Oiseau S-298

Concert in D major, Op. 21
  Louis Kaufman, Violin
  Arthur Balsam, Piano
  The Pascal Quartet
	Orion 73134

A Russian recording of the same work:
  M. Lubotsky, Violin
  L. Edlina, Piano
  The Borodin Quartet
	Melodiya 33CM

Poème de l'amour et de la mer, Op. 19
  Victoria de los Angeles
  Lamoureux Concerts Orchestra,
  Jean-Pierre Jacquillat
	Angel S-36897

Poème, Op. 25
  Francescatti, New York Philharmonic,
    Bernstein
	Col. MS-6617

Grumiaux, Lamoureux, Rosenthal	Philips 802708
Milstein, Fistoulari	Angel S-36005
D. Oistrakh, Boston Symphony, Munch	RCA VICS-1058
I. Oistrakh, Moscow Radio Symphony, Rozhdestvensky	Mel./Ang. S-40077

Perlman, Paris Conservatory Orchestra, Martinon	Angel S-37118
Rosand, SW German Radio Orchestra, Reinhardt	Turnabout 34466
Zukerman, London Symphony, Mackerras	Col. MS-7422
Quartet in A major, Op. 30 (Piano) Richards Piano Quartet	Oiseau S-316
Quartet in C minor, Op. 35 (String) Via Nova Quartet	MHS 1351Z
Quelques danses, Op. 26	
Jean Doyen, Piano	MHS 1155Z/1157T
Johannesen, Piano (collection)	3-VOXSVBX-5483
Pleshakov, Piano	Orion 6906
Symphony in B-flat major, Op. 20	
Detroit Symphony, Paray	Mercury 75029
Paris Conservatory Orchestra, Denzler	London STS-15145
Suisse Romande, Ansermet	London STS-15294

Bibliography

ARTICLES, DICTIONARIES, ENCYCLOPEDIAS, AND PERIODICALS

Bacou, Roseline. "Décors d'appartements au temps des Nabis," *Art de France* 4 (1964): 190–205.

Bénézit, Emmanuel, ed. *Dictionnaire des Peintres, Sculpteurs, Dessinateurs et Graveurs.* 8 vols. Paris: Libraire Grund, 1954.

Bouchor, Maurice. "Le Langage et l'esprit," *La Revue Musicale,* December 1, 1925, pp. 180–90.

Brailoïu, Constantin. "Pentatony in Debussy's Music," *Studia Memoriae Belae Bartók Sacra,* 3d ed., London: Boosey and Hawkes, Ltd., 1959, 377–417.

Bréville, Pierre de. "Ernest Chausson," *Mercure de France* 31 (September 1899): 687–94.

————. "Les Fioretti du Père Franck," *Mercure de France* 262 (September 1, 1935): 244–63.

Calvocoressi, M. D. "A la mémoire d'Ernest Chausson," *l'Art Moderne* 23 (May 24, 1903): 189–90.

————. "Le Roi Arthus d'Ernest Chausson," *Guide Musical* 49 (October 18, 1903): 703–8.

Carraud, Gaston. "Ernest Chausson," *Le Ménestrel* 82 (April 2, 1920): 137–39.

"Correspondance inédite de Claude Debussy et Ernest Chausson," *La Revue Musicale,* December 1, 1925, pp. 116–26.

Crankshaw, Geoffrey. "The Songs of Chausson," *The Monthly Musical Record* 83 (July–August 1953): 148–51.

Dubois, Anthony. "Ernest Chausson," *Guide Musical* 45 (July 2, 1899): 516–17.

Du Bos, Charles. "Chausson et la consolation par le coeur," *La Revue Musicale,* December 1, 1925, pp. 99–107.

Duthuit, Georges. "Vuillard and the Poets of Decadence," *Art News* 53, no. 1 (March 1954): 29.

Feschotte, Jacques. "Ernest Chausson et la poésie," *Musica,* September 1957, pp. 2–5.

Hallays, André. "Le Roi Arthus," *Revue de Paris* 6 (December 15, 1903): 846–58.

Hoerée, Arthur. "Chausson et la musique française," *La Revue Musicale,* December 1, 1925, pp. 191–206.

Indy, Vincent d'. "César Franck," *Cyclopedic Survey of Chamber Music.* Compiled and edited by Walter Willson Cobbett. Vol. 1. 2d ed. London: Oxford University Press, 1963. Pp. 418–29.

———. "Ernest Chausson," *Cyclopedic Survey of Chamber Music.* Compiled and edited by Walter Willson Cobbett. Vol. 1. 2d ed. London: Oxford University Press, 1963. Pp. 266–70.

Jean-Aubry, G. "A French Composer: Ernest Chausson," *The Musical Times* 59 (November 1, 1918): 500–1.

Lesure, François. "Claude Debussy, Ernest Chausson et Henri Lerolle," *Humanisme actif* (Paris, 1968), 337–44.

"Lettres de Henri Duparc à Ernest Chausson," *Revue de Musicologie* 38 (December 1956): 125–46.

"Lettres inédites à Mme de Rayssac," *La Revue Musicale,* December 1, 1925, pp. 137–42.

"Lettres inédites à Paul Poujaud," *La Revue Musicale,* December 1, 1925, pp. 143–74.

"Lettres inédites à Vincent d'Indy," *La Revue Musicale,* December 1, 1925, pp. 128–36.

Lockspeiser, Edward. "The French Song in the Nineteenth Century," *The Musical Quarterly* 26 (April 1940): 192–99.

Mauclair, Camille. "Souvenirs sur Ernest Chausson," *La Vogue* 3 (August 15, 1899): 73–82.

Maus, Octave. "Ernest Chausson," *l'Art Moderne* 19 (June 18, 1899): 205–7.

Oulmont, Charles. "Deux amis, Claude Debussy et Ernest Chausson. Documents inédits," *Mercure de France* 256 (December 1, 1934): 248–69.

Philpott, A. R. *Dictionary of Puppetry.* Boston: Plays, Inc., 1969.

Polignac, Princesse Edmond de. "Memoirs of the Late Princesse Edmond de Polignac," *Horizon* 12, no. 68 (August 1945): 110–41.

"Quelques opinions sur Ernest Chausson," *La Revue Musicale,* December 1, 1925, pp. 207–16.

Samazeuilh, Gustave. "Ernest Chausson," *La Revue Musicale,* December 1, 1925, pp. 108–15.

————. "Ernest Chausson et le 'Roi Arthus,'" *La Revue Musicale,* December 15, 1903, pp. 699–705.

Schaeffner, André. "Sur quelques caractères de l'influence Franckiste," *La Revue Musicale,* December 1, 1922, pp. 142–54.

Servières, Georges. "Lieder français, Ernest Chausson," *Guide Musical* 43 (December 19, 1897): 843–46.

Tiersot, Julien. "Ernest Chausson," *Guide Musical* 45 (June 25, 1899): 503–4.

Wye, Benjamin Van. "Gregorian Influences in French Organ Music Before the *Motu proprio,*" JAMS 27, no. 1 (Spring 1974): 1–24.

BOOKS

Abraham, Gerald. *A Hundred Years of Music.* 2d ed. London: Duckworth, 1949.

Almendra, Julia d'. *Les Modes grégoriens dans l'oeuvre de Claude Debussy.* Paris: 1947.

Bacou, Roseline. *Odilon Redon.* Geneva: Pierre Cailler, 1956.

Balakian, Anna. *The Symbolist Movement: A Critical Appraisal.* New York: Random House, 1967.

Barricelli, Jean-Pierre, and Weinstein, Leo. *Ernest Chausson: The Composer's Life and Works.* Norman: University of Oklahoma Press, 1955.

Bernard, Suzanne. *Mallarmé et la musique.* Paris: Libraire Nizet, 1959.

Borren, Charles van den. *César Franck.* Brussels: La Renaissance du Livre, 1950.

Bowra, C. M. *The Heritage of Symbolism.* London: Macmillan & Co., Ltd., 1947.

Chassé, Charles. *The Nabis and Their Period.* Translated by Michael Bullock. New York: Frederick A. Praeger, 1969.

Cooper, Martin. *French Music: From the Death of Berlioz to the Death of Fauré.* London: Oxford University Press, 1951.

Cortot, Alfred. *La Musique française de piano.* Vol. 1. 5th ed. Paris: Presses Universitaires de France, 1948.

Crespelle, Jean-Paul. *The Fauves.* Greenwich: New York Graphic Society, 1962.

————. *Les Maîtres de la belle époque.* Paris: Hachette, 1966.

Crist, Bainbridge. *The Art of Setting Words to Music.* New York: Carl Fischer, Inc., 1944.

Davies, Laurence. *César Franck and His Circle.* Boston: Houghton Mifflin Co., 1970.

Demuth, Norman. *César Franck.* London: Dennis Dobson, Ltd., 1949.

_____. *French Piano Music: A Survey With Notes On Its Performance.* London: Museum Press, 1959.

_____. *Vincent d'Indy, Champion of Classicism.* London: Rockliff, 1951.

Denis, Maurice. *Henri Lerolle et ses amis.* Paris: 1932.

_____. *Journal* (1884–1904). Vol. 1. Paris: La Colombe, 1957.

Emmanuel, Maurice. *César Franck.* Paris: Libraire Renouard, 1930.

_____. *Pelléas et Mélisande de Claude Debussy.* Paris: Libraire Delaplane, n.d.

France, Anatole. *La Vie littéraire.* Vols. 2 and 3. Paris: Calmann-Lévy, 1907.

Gallois, Jean. *Ernest Chausson: L'homme et son oeuvre.* Paris: Éditions Seghers, 1967.

_____. *César Franck.* Paris: Éditions du Seuil, 1966.

Grout, Donald Jay. *A History of Western Music.* Rev. ed. New York: W. W. Norton and Co., Inc., 1973.

_____. *A Short History of Opera.* New York: Columbia University Press, 1947.

Halls, W. D. *Maurice Maeterlinck: Study of His Life and Thought.* London: Oxford University Press, 1960.

Henderson, John A. *The First Avant-Garde* (1887–1894), London: George G. Harrap & Co., Ltd., 1971.

Hill, Edward Burlingame. *Modern French Music.* Boston: Houghton Mifflin Co., 1924.

Hofstätter, Hans H. *Geschichte der europäischen Jugendstilmalerei.* Köln: M. DuMont Schauberg, 1963.

_____. *Symbolismus und die Kunst der Jahrhundert.* Köln: M. DuMont Schauberg, 1965.

Humbert, Agnès. *Les Nabis et leur époque, 1888–1900.* Geneva: Pierre Cailler, 1954.

Indy, Vincent d'. *César Franck.* Translated by Rosa Newmarch. London: The Bodley Head Ltd., 1909.

_____. *Cours de composition musicale.* 3 vols. Paris: Durand et Cie., 1950.

_____ . *Richard Wagner et son influence sur l'art musical français.* Paris: Delagrave, 1930.

Jamot, Paul. *Maurice Denis.* Paris: 1945.

Jean-Aubry, G. *French Music of Today.* Translated by Edwin Evans. London: Kegan Paul, Trench, Trubner & Co., Ltd., 1926.

Kahn, Gustave. *Fantin-Latour.* Paris: F. Rieder & Cie., 1926.

Kurth, Ernst. *Romantische Harmonik und ihre Krise in Wagners "Tristan."* 2d ed. Berlin: M. Hesse, 1923.

Landormy, Paul. *La Musique française de Franck à Debussy.* 11th ed. Paris: Libraire Gallimard, 1943.

Lang, Paul Henry. *Music in Western Civilization.* New York: W. W. Norton and Co., Inc., 1941.

Lavignac, Albert. *Voyage artistique à Bayreuth.* Paris: Albin Michel, 1903.

Lehmann, A. G. *The Symbolist Aesthetic in France: 1885-1895.* Oxford: Basil Blackwell, 1950.

Lockspeiser, Edward. *Debussy.* New York: Pellegrini and Cudahy Inc., 1949.

_____ . *Debussy: His Life and Mind.* Vol. 1: 1862-1902. London: Cassell, 1962.

Madsen, S. Tschudi. *Art Nouveau.* Translated by R. I. Christopherson. New York: McGraw-Hill Book Co., 1967.

Martino, Pierre. *Parnasse et Symbolisme.* 10th ed. Paris: Libraire Armand Colin, 1958.

Mauclair, Camille. *Le Soleil des morts: roman contemporain.* Paris: Paul Ollendorff, 1898.

Mellerio, André. *Odilon Redon, peintre, dessinateur et graveur.* Paris: Floury, 1923.

Michaud, Guy. *Mallarmé.* Translated by Marie Collins and Bertha Humez. New York: New York University Press, 1965.

Myers, Rollo H. *Erik Satie.* New York: Dover Publications, Inc., 1968.

Nichols, Roger. *Debussy.* London: Oxford University Press, 1973.

Northcote, Sydney. *The Songs of Henri Duparc.* London: Dennis Dobson, Ltd., 1949.

Noske, Frits. *French Song From Berlioz to Duparc.* Translated by Rita Benton. 2d ed., rev. Rita Benton and Frits Noske, New York: Dover Publications, Inc., 1970.

Oulmont, Charles. *Musique de l'amour.* 2 vols. Paris: Desclée de Brouwer & Cie., 1935.

Perry, Carl David. "The Songs of Henri Duparc." Unpublished Master's thesis, Department of Music, University of North Carolina, 1955.

Poulenc, Francis. *Emmanuel Chabrier.* Paris: La Palatine, 1961.

Richardson, Joanna. *Verlaine.* New York: The Viking Press, 1971.

Sandström, Sven. *Le Monde imaginaire d'Odilon Redon.* Translated into French from the Swedish by Denise Naert. Lund: 1955.

Senior, John. *The Way Down and Out: The Occult in Symbolist Literature.* Ithaca: Cornell University Press, 1959.

Seroff, Victor I. *Debussy: Musician of France.* New York: G. P. Putnam's Sons, 1956.

Shattuck, Roger. *The Banquet Years.* New York: Harcourt, Brace & Co., 1958.

Stevens, Denis, ed. *A History of Song.* New York: W. W. Norton and Co., Inc., 1961.

Swart, Koenraad W. *The Sense of Decadence in Nineteenth-Century France.* The Hague: Martinus Nijhoff, 1964.

Thompson, Oscar. *Debussy: Man and Artist.* New York: Tudor Publishing Co., 1940.

Tiersot, Julien. *Un Demi-siècle de musique française: Entre les deux guerres, 1870–1917.* Paris: F. Alcan, 1918.

Tovey, Donald Francis. *Essays in Musical Analysis.* Vol. 2. London: Oxford University Press, 1935.

Vallas, Léon. *César Franck.* Translated by Hubert Foss. New York: Oxford University Press, 1951.

————. *Claude Debussy.* Translated by Maire and Grace O'Brien. London: Oxford University Press, 1933.

————. *Claude Debussy et son temps.* Paris: F. Alcan, 1932.

————. *The Theories of Claude Debussy.* Translated by Maire O'Brien. London: Oxford University Press, 1929.

————. *Vincent d'Indy.* 2 vols. Paris: A. Michel, 1946 and 1950.

Vogel, Martin. *Der Tristan-Akkord und die Krise der modernen Harmonie-Lehre:* Band 2 der *Orpheus*—Schriftenreihe zu Grundfragen der Musik. Düsseldorf: Gesellschaft zur Förderung der systematischen Musikwissenschaft, 1962.

Wilson, Edmund. *Axel's Castle.* New York: Charles Scribner's Sons, 1932.

Zuckerman, Elliott. *The First Hundred Years of Wagner's Tristan.* New York: Columbia University Press, 1964.

Zweig, Paul. *The Heresy of Self-Love.* New York: Basic Books, Inc., 1968.

Index